Subediting for Journalists

Subediting for Journalists is a concise, up-to-date and readable introduction to the skills of subediting for newspapers and magazines. It describes how subediting developed, from the early days of printing to the modern era of computers and the internet, and explains clearly what the sub now has to do.

Using practical examples from newspapers and magazines, *Subediting for Journalists* introduces the various techniques involved in subediting from cutting copy to writing captions and coverlines. *Subediting for Journalists* includes:

- House style explained with a model stylebook provided
- Examples of bad journalistic English
- Subbing news and features for sense and style
- Editing quotes and readers' letters
- Writing headlines and standfirsts
- Making copy legally safe
- Understanding production, using software packages and website subbing
- A glossary of journalistic terms and notes on further reading.

Wynford Hicks is a freelance journalist and editorial trainer. He is the author of *English for Journalists* and *Writing for Journalists* and a contributor to *Interviewing for Journalists*, all published by Routledge.

Tim Holmes is a freelance journalist and former magazine publisher. He teaches and researches magazine journalism at the Centre for Journalism Studies, Cardiff University.

Media Skills

SERIES EDITOR: RICHARD KEEBLE, CITY UNIVERSITY, LONDON
SERIES ADVISERS: WYNFORD HICKS AND JENNY MCKAY

The *Media Skills* series provides a concise and thorough introduction to a rapidly changing media landscape. Each book is written by media and journalism lecturers or experienced professionals and is a key resource for a particular industry. Offering helpful advice and information and using practical examples from print, broadcast and digital media, as well as discussing ethical and regulatory issues, *Media Skills* books are essential guides for students and media professionals.

Also in this series:

English for Journalists, 2nd edition
Wynford Hicks

Writing for Journalists
Wynford Hicks with Sally Adams and Harriett Gilbert

Interviewing for Radio
Jim Beaman

Web Production for Writers and Journalists, 2nd edition
Jason Whittaker

Ethics for Journalists
Richard Keeble

Scriptwriting for the Screen
Charlie Moritz

Interviewing for Journalists
Sally Adams, with an introduction and additional material by Wynford Hicks

Researching for Television and Radio
Adèle Emm

Reporting for Journalists
Chris Frost

Find more details of current *Media Skills* books and forthcoming titles at
www.producing.routledge.com

Subediting for Journalists

Wynford Hicks and
Tim Holmes

London and New York

First published 2002
by Routledge
11 New Fetter Lane, London EC4P 4EE

Simultaneously published in the USA and Canada
by Routledge
29 West 35th Street, New York, NY 10001

Routledge is an imprint of the Taylor & Francis Group

Typeset in Goudy Oldstyle by
Florence Production Ltd, Stoodleigh, Devon
Printed and bound in Great Britain by
Biddles Ltd, Guildford and King's Lynn

British Library Cataloguing in Publication Data
A catalogue record for this book is available from the British Library

Library of Congress Cataloging in Publication Data
Hicks, Wynford, 1942–
  Subediting for journalists/Wynford Hicks and Tim Holmes.
    p. cm. — (Media skills)
  Includes bibliographical references and index.
  1. Journalism—Editing. I. Holmes, Tim, 1953–   II. Title. III. Series.
PN4778.H48 2002
070.4′1—dc21   2002024908

ISBN 0–415–24084–0 (hbk)
ISBN 0–415–24085–9 (pbk)

Contents

Figures

Acknowledgements

This book owes much to our colleagues – journalists, students and fellow tutors. In particular we would like to thank:

The *Guardian* and its readers' editor, Ian Mayes, for permission to reprint his Open door piece on Billy the Kid.

Mike Woof, Bernard Eccles and Ronan Quinlan for permission to reprint their contributions to the *Journalist*'s Chief sub column – and editor Tim Gopsill for running the column, in which some of the material in this book was first published.

David Marsh of the *Guardian* for reading the proofs and Richard Jell for his additions to the glossary.

The many graduates of Cardiff University who replied with grace and speed to a flurry of emails inquiring about their working practices. Special thanks to Will Ham Bevan and Paul Dring for their contributions.

Pat English for keeping an open line as she guided the *Western Mail* from flat plan to printing press.

Authors' note

If you find a mistake in this book – or have any comment or suggestion to make – please get in touch. But to save you the trouble of writing to us about the title, we are aware that the phrase 'Subediting for Journalists' conflicts with a basic principle of subediting – that is, never say more than you need. For subediting is done in newspaper and magazine offices, not cafeterias and call centres, and by journalists, not accountants. Other people edit documents; only journalists sub copy.

But *Subediting for Journalists* is part of the *Media Skills* series – it follows *English for Journalists*, *Writing for Journalists* and *Interviewing for Journalists* and is intended to complement them. The title makes this clear.

Because this book is part of a series it does not set out to cover everything that a subeditor needs to know. For example, it does not repeat the rules of grammar (*English for Journalists*) or the basics of news writing (*Writing for Journalists*). Nor does it cover design and layout, which will be the subject of a separate book in the series.

Wynford Hicks
hicks@mageos.com

Tim Holmes
holmesta@cf.ac.uk

1
Introduction

> ## WANTED: SUBEDITOR
>
> Must have traditional subbing skills, excellent spelling and grammar, be good at rewrites and converting to house style, capable of coming up with great headlines, standfirsts and captions, generally computer literate but an expert at layout using QuarkXPress, with management skills and the expertise to oversee the entire production process from raw copy to final pages. Experience of online journalism and web pages would be an advantage, as would the ability to write news and features. Must also be fast, accurate, legally aware and able to cope under pressure.
>
> Oh, and must not mind being invisible in the final product or having the job dismissed as desk-bound drudgery.

It seems like a lot to ask of one job – and it is. Yet all these desired qualities were derived from advertisements for subediting jobs in either *Press Gazette* or *Media Guardian*; if nothing else, this demonstrates that the list of skills required of a subeditor is broad and still growing.

Looking at these trends as opportunities rather than threats, there is probably more scope than ever before for anyone who wants to enter journalism as a subeditor, but how did a job which was long seen as a backroom speciality come to be so inclusive?

Background

Leslie Sellers begins his classic handbook *The Simple Subs Book* by deprecating the practice of starting with a historical overview. 'Subeditors,' he wrote, 'haven't any history to speak of. Their arrival on the scene is due to two factors – the size and complexity of modern newspaper organisations, and the increasing concentration on both readability and design.'

Good as his book is, he was wrong on two counts, for the subeditor's craft can be traced from the birth of modern printing processes right through to the latest desktop publishing systems, a period of at least 500 years. And since Sellers wrote that, there have been numerous technological advances, each of which has added a new layer to the subeditor's duties as well as altering the commercial and economic basis of the publishing industry.

This cumulative development makes it difficult to pin down what exactly is expected of a subeditor. Nor is the job description static; look through *Media Guardian* on a Monday and alongside the advertisements for subeditors you will find firms looking for 'production editors', who have a very similar role but with the added responsibility of keeping the publication on schedule.

As for what subs do, there has, as one old hand noted in the 1960s, long been confusion over this: 'I can remember when schoolmasters used to approach newspapers for holiday jobs as subeditors. They thought the work would involve no more than correcting errors of grammar and spelling. Would that it were so easy!'

Subeditors certainly must correct spelling and grammar, but they must also check factual accuracy, rewrite copy to make it better or to fit in with a house style, seek out potential libels and remove them, fit copy into a layout, and devise headlines, standfirsts and captions. They may have to lay copy out on the page having selected, cropped and sized the illustrations or photographs. All of this will probably be done at a computer screen using a panoply of software packages, each of which the subeditor must be able to use, although wise subs will still leave some room on their desks for paper.

This is a condensed summary of a subeditor's tasks, from the beginning to the end. Not, please note, from the trivial to the essential. Ensuring that a piece of copy is spelt correctly is at least as important as putting that copy into a layout – and it was with spelling that it all started.

The subeditor's job had its beginnings around 1450, when the German goldsmith Johann Gutenberg successfully developed the use of movable type. Contrary to popular belief, he did not invent printing as such. 'What was epoch-making in Gutenberg's process was the possibility of editing and correcting a text which was then (at least in theory) identical in every copy; in other words, mass production preceded by critical proofreading,' according to Saul Steinberg in his standard history of printing. It is also worth noting that Gutenberg simultaneously invented typography, the art of making and using typefaces – a topic in which subeditors will have a natural interest.

Creating two modern industries with a single development is remarkable enough, but a third was also made possible, and it was the one which is of most interest to us as professional journalists:

At the same time, when Gutenberg made it feasible to put on the market a large number of identical copies at any given time, he thereby fore-shadowed the possibility of ever increasing the number of copies and ever reducing the length of time needed for their issue ... Thus Gutenberg can be acclaimed also as the progenitor of the periodical press.

(S. H. Steinberg, *Five Hundred Years of Printing*, p. 7)

Once the possibility of making corrections to texts had been established, editing could begin in earnest, and with some academic prestige attached to it. One Swiss printer of the 15th century employed only university professors as editors.

With proofreading firmly incorporated, the next step was to ensure uniformity in the use of language. William Caxton decided to adopt the dialect of London and the Home Counties for books such as *The Canterbury Tales* (1478), and his successor Wynkyn de Worde (a true subeditor's name if ever there was one) developed the process to such an extent that he could 'put forward a modest claim to having inaugurated what we now call the house style of a printing or publishing firm, which overrides the inconsistencies of individual authors' (Steinberg, p. 58).

Technical advances in printing and typography changed the way books, pamphlets, circulars, periodicals and newspapers looked, but the next major advance came from a printer, publisher and journalist of the 18th century. John Bell revolutionised the look of the English newspaper. He was the first to realise that a newspaper is read quickly, unlike a book, and he drew the typographical conclusions. The pages of his newspapers were laid out in columns, and they emphasised the paragraph as centre of the newspaper-reader's interest. Bell started numerous newspapers, and his son John Browne Bell also founded a number, the best known of which is the *News of the World*, born in 1843 and still going strong.

Thus, by the beginning of the 19th century, the subeditor's domain already incorporated spelling, grammar, house style and eye-catching layout even if the job title had not become common currency. Well before any modern news-paper had been organised, there was a concentration on readability and design.

Subediting news

When the modern newspaper organisation did arrive, it could draw on a long-established body of expertise. The history of newspapers has been covered by many scholars and does not need to be repeated here, except to note that the modern era is generally agreed to have begun with the launch of the *Daily Mail* in 1896.

The man behind the *Mail*, Alfred Harmsworth (later Viscount Northcliffe), achieved his first publishing success with a magazine called *Answers*, based on the idea of replying to inquiries from readers about all sorts of topics. The answers were short, snappy, factual and plentiful, mixed in with competitions to attract and keep readers. This technique found its way into the *Daily Mail*, where the single-paragraph items that had dominated *Answers* were adapted to the business of reporting news.

Clearly it is a skilled job to condense news reports into bite-sized chunks which will still tell the story accurately, and this is when newspaper subeditors began to come into their own. The *Times* and the *Daily Telegraph* had been content to run columns and columns of verbatim reports from parliament or the courts (as much as 61,500 words on occasion), leading to dense blocks of type made even less readable by pompous writing styles.

The *Daily Mail* cut through all this to present news in a format which could be easily taken in by people commuting from the suburbs. One consequence was that power passed from reporters paid by the word to deskbound subeditors who could literally cut their prose down to size. The saying that 'reporters have all the glamour but subeditors have all the power' might well be traced back to 4 May 1896.

Since then, the characteristics of a subeditor have been more-or-less taken for granted. They include a sense of news values and command of the language, quickness of thought coupled with accuracy, judgment based on well-informed common sense, knowledge of the main principles of the laws of libel, contempt and copyright, a comprehensive technical knowledge of production processes – and the unusual attribute of seeing both sides of an argument.

As for what a sub actually does, *Guardian* readers' editor Ian Mayes says:

> It is the subeditor who checks the reporter's copy for grammatical and, so far as it is possible, factual errors. A sub is not expected to reresearch a story or, indeed, to carry out research where insufficient appears to have been done. It is the subeditor who cuts copy to the required size (a creative skill not to be undervalued), writes headlines and captions and, in certain cases, who lays out the page, articulating the headings, stories, pictures and graphics to reflect his/her or the section editor's priorities in a structure of asymmetrical balance.
>
> In the end the page has to look good, to convey the weight and sense of its contents clearly, and to provide a text free from linguistic obstacles. Subbing may be a sedentary occupation but it is not a passive one . . . It is one of those occupations in which a measure of success is the degree to which the practitioner is rendered invisible.
>
> (*Guardian Saturday Review*, 18 September 1999)

Subediting features

One notable way in which newspapers have changed over the last few years has been the inclusion of more features, more 'magazine-y' material – and indeed more magazines as part of Saturday and Sunday packages. And if newspapers have changed, magazines led the way.

Up to this point the main focus has been the role of the news subeditor, which would apply equally to news-oriented periodicals, especially trade weeklies. Features, however, require different treatment. To take two possible extremes, the words may have been commissioned from a writer who has a great style but no in-depth knowledge of the subject, or, conversely, from an expert with no writing skills. Either scenario is entirely possible, as acknowledged by John Morrish in his book *Magazine Editing*: 'The craft of the subeditor is absolutely vital to successful magazine journalism, which increasingly relies on the seamless incorporation of copy from many different writers.'

He then specifies the magazine sub's role:

> Subediting has three strands: a kind of quality control, ensuring that everything is accurate, well-written and likely to be legally safe; a production function, ensuring that everything fits and that deadlines are kept; and a key role in the projection of material, through the writing of appropriate and attention-grabbing headlines, standfirsts and captions.

Exactly the same range of tasks applies to subediting features for newspapers.

Recent developments: newspapers

Despite the changes mentioned above there still seems to be widespread agreement on what it means to be a newspaper subeditor. Analysis of the advertisements in *Press Gazette* and *Media Guardian* shows that newspapers are generally happy to specify just the job title without further qualification; anyone suitable for the job, it is implied, will already know what a subeditor on the *Oxford Courier* or a news subeditor on the *Birmingham Post* is expected to do.

This contrasts strongly with advertisements for posts on magazines, which tend to ask for particular skills and personal characteristics. It also runs contrary to the news which *Press Gazette* reports. The newspaper industry has not, in fact, remained static for the last 100 years, or even the last 10; new technology and cost-cutting have had far-reaching effects on the way all journalists are expected to do their jobs, and there has been considerable debate over the position subediting should occupy in a newspaper's organisation.

The development of increasingly powerful and sophisticated computer layout packages – with the greatly diminished power of the graphical and print unions – has allowed journalists to take over typesetting and layout. Thus subeditors subsumed the role of at least one and possibly two departments or contractors; typesetters and compositors may have retrained as layout artists when the skills of scalpel and steel rule were still required, but their new jobs would have lasted only as long as it took screen-based page design systems to conquer the publishing world.

But the changes have not stopped there. The former *Mirror* editor David Montgomery said in a 1997 speech to the World Newspaper Congress and World Editors Forum: 'Many of the structures that were created in the hot-metal days of the 1930s still survive. The technology of the 1980s, as it became widespread, was simply imposed on top of those old structures . . . When the screens arrived not a lot changed.'

Montgomery's idea was that all journalists should be trained in a number of skills and would take up roles as either writers or page editors. Of subeditors he said:

> The modern subeditorial function was conceived in the 1930s. Sixty years later it is no longer appropriate to employ single-skilled text editors, or people who have little function but to cut copy to length.
>
> The technology and screen skills of the journalist should enable the modern subeditor to be, in fact, a fully fledged editor. This modern-style journalist can select stories, put them in order of prominence, design the page, write the headlines, put in and manipulate the pictures, edit the text, review the work in total and send the page to the printer. This effectively eliminates four or five departments . . . [and] inevitably means the death of the subeditor and the birth of the page editor.
>
> (*Press Gazette*, 13 June 1997)

I have quoted Montgomery at some length because subsequent correspondence in *Press Gazette* showed he was articulating what had already become standard practice at a number of local and regional newspapers. 'If he wants to see his vision of the future in action, he is welcome to visit us,' said the editor of the *Ealing Gazette and Leader*; and in the following weeks first the *Hull Daily Mail*, then the Midland Independent Newspapers (MIN) group and finally the *European* revealed new production structures which were more or less identical to Montgomery's outline.

This vision of how a modern newspaper should organise its production systems found adherents elsewhere, although the job titles sometimes differed. When *Express* editor Richard Addis found it necessary to cut 19 production jobs after the introduction of Quark Publishing System (QPS), he tried to present it as a return to tradition:

> I am increasing the power of subeditors again, restoring them to their rightful position ... Subeditors used to be the gods of newspapers, particularly at the *Express* 20 years ago, and they have gradually had parts of their skill removed and given to other people – design, pictures, imaging departments, the back bench.

> With the right subs and the best quality subs, it will be a good thing to have them doing design, headlines, captions and full pages.

(But did this happen? See Chapter 2.)

Is there a uniform conclusion to be drawn from this slightly fragmented picture? The most likely one seems to be that production processes will continue to be affected by technological advances which will lead to different working practices, skill requirements and job descriptions. Quark Publishing System is often mentioned in reports of job losses, but that particular software package is just another stop on a road embarked upon back in the 1970s, when hot-metal typesetting gave way to phototypesetting (see Chapter 12).

Recent developments: periodicals

Periodicals have not been entirely sheltered from the winds of change. Even though magazines have evolved production hierarchies which are generally more streamlined and multi-skilled than those in newspapers and adopted computer technology earlier and more thoroughly, some managers have been tempted to tweak the system further. In February 1996 the editor of the women's weekly *Bella*, Jackie Highe, announced that they would henceforth be relying on 'copy fitters' to match words to layouts, with writers subbing their own work. Her memo included the line 'This involves removing the subs department', and an insider reported that 'subbing duties are being imposed on department heads', most of whom had no relevant computer experience.

One response to this news came from the chief subeditor of the *Health Service Journal* who enumerated all the benefits a good subeditor brings to a title. To summarise, subs can help to keep readers reading, improve dull stories, pick up errors, excise libels and, in short, act as 'a reporter, an editor, a designer and a proofreader all rolled into one'. As the buffer between writer and reader they should be 'the linchpins of the modern editorial process'.

Before the end of the year *Bella*'s editor had changed her mind about the value (and cost) of subs. *Press Gazette* reported that Highe had offered an experienced subeditor a job as 'chief text editor' but had then withdrawn the offer in favour of 'plan A ... the continental system of having a dedicated subeditor in each department'.

Note that not even *Bella* wanted to make the 'copyfitters' or writers do the layouts. Because of the highly stylised nature of magazines it is still common for them to have their own designers or art editors, although smaller operations and more news-oriented weeklies may rely on subeditors or production editors to lay out some sections. (The very smallest magazines will probably rely on everyone doing everything, and 'everyone' may well mean 'one'.)

The future of subediting

Despite all of the above, there are signs that web publishing, far from abolishing the need for subeditors, will actually enhance the role and its skills, even if under a different name. Although the sector will be in a state of flux for some time, jobs for website 'producers' incorporate many of the duties of a subeditor (see Chapter 13).

Text on websites is usually very condensed, giving plenty of scope for skilful copy editing. On top of this, the web is a very visual medium which readers navigate in a different way from physical publications; understanding what readers want and where and how they want to see it is seen as a key to success, which is why Danny Meadows-Klue of the *Electronic Telegraph* told *Press Gazette*: 'Subbing will become the battleground for new media . . . The art of the sub is to take copy and decide what they can do to make it relevant to the medium. They will decide where copy will go and what it will become.'

Data management, the speed of reaction which the internet demands and evolving technological requirements will continue to cause the production process, and thus the subeditor's job, to change. The good news is that, no matter what medium journalism is delivered through, subediting skills will always be in demand.

Tim Holmes

2
Working methods

Let's start with a joke.

> A man in a hot-air balloon realised he was lost. He reduced altitude and spotted a woman below. He descended a bit more and shouted: 'Excuse me, can you help me? I promised a friend I would meet him an hour ago, but I don't know where I am.'

> The woman below replied: 'You are in a hot air balloon hovering approximately 30 feet above the ground. You are between 40 and 41 degrees north latitude and between 59 and 60 degrees west longitude.'

> 'You must be a chief subeditor,' said the balloonist.

> 'I am,' replied the woman, 'but how did you know?'

> 'Well,' answered the balloonist, 'everything you told me is technically correct, but I have no idea what to make of your information, and the fact is I'm still lost. Frankly, you've not been much help so far.'

> The woman below responded: 'You must be a writer.'

> 'I am,' replied the balloonist, 'but how did you know?'

> 'Well,' said the woman, 'you don't know where you are or where you are going. You have risen to where you are thanks to a large quantity of hot air. You made a promise which you have no idea how to keep, and you expect me to solve your problem. The fact is, you are in exactly the same position you were in before, but now, somehow, it's my fault.'

Like most jokes, this one includes elements of truth and if some of them can be teased out it might help to explain what is involved in a subeditor's work.

First of all, you need to be aware of the most mundane, banal facts ('You are in a hot air balloon . . .'). It is easy to overlook the obvious, especially when you're in a hurry and there's a deadline approaching. Make sure of the ground beneath your feet before rushing to complete a job.

Then you need to apply more detailed knowledge ('latitude and longitude'); this might require you to check facts, names or figures in the copy. It is important for a subeditor to have a wide range of information to hand, but it is also important to admit when you don't know something. Then you can turn to reference books, reliable sources on the internet, or phone the person named to check.

Finally, you must be prepared to accept the blame if something goes wrong and to be completely overlooked if it all goes right.

Analysing a joke and drawing metaphorical lessons are all very well, but what does all this mean in practice? What is the best way to set about your work as a subeditor?

As with any craft job there are certain tools required. A sub will do well to be equipped with a fine red pen, a ruler, filing trays, a fully functional computer, a spelling dictionary, a sub's dictionary, a copy of your publication's house style, a thesaurus and miscellaneous reference books relevant to the publication's subject area.

If that sounds like a lot, it is in fact the minimum. On top of that you must know how to use everything in that list, especially the computer. This does not just mean knowing how to boot it up and get into the word-processing package.

Know how to get at the copy

In days gone by this might have meant shouting for the copy boy, locating your in-tray or opening an envelope. For most subeditors, however, it is likely to mean something more electro-mechanical.

Copy comes in many forms, ranging from the traditional marks on paper through a variety of computer storage devices to a series of 1s and 0s encoded by software. Dealing with copy from in-house journalists should be straightforward if everyone is using an integrated system or network of computers. Copy from external sources can sometimes present more of a challenge.

If it is on paper, it must – eventually – be transferred to screen, which may mean typing it in yourself. However, there is one advantage to this format: most people still find it easier and more accurate to sub on hard copy than on screen, so you can get to grips with the raw text before transferring it.

Copy on disk should present no problems, provided that a) you have access to a machine that will read that kind of disk, and b) the writer has used a form of software compatible with yours. Both of these things should have been clearly specified before the writer submitted anything.

Material may also come as compressed email attachments which may not survive digital transmission in exactly the same format they were sent. For example, a document which has been composed on a PC may, when opened on a Macintosh, have strange characters instead of quote marks or apostrophes, not to mention pages and pages of digi-nonsense appended. The sub's first job must be to clean up the copy and if you don't know how to search and replace effectively it's going to take you a long time. That's assuming you have been able to unzip the attachment in the first place.

While your employer should take a certain responsibility for ensuring that you are familiar with or trained up in whatever system is in use, it is largely up to you to become better acquainted with it. No one likes being constantly interrupted by a newcomer who can't get on with the computer, so resolve now never to be that person.

Know what to do with the copy when you've got it

When you have the copy in front of you, you can start to work on it. If it is not in hard copy form already, bear in mind that many experienced subeditors prefer, if possible, to read a piece from paper rather than from a screen; it seems that, for the time being, the human eye and brain find it easier to scan solid processed tree than a flickering collection of points of light. So get a printout if necessary and clear enough space on your desk to spread it out.

This is where the ruler comes in: it's not to draw straight rules but to help you read proofs line by line and avoid skipping over sections. The fine pen is for writing neatly between lines and in margins. You might also consider wearing earplugs if your office is noisy – anything to aid concentration because that's what you will need from now on.

Your tasks will be to make sure that:

- the piece deals with what the writer was asked to deal with
- it will make sense to the reader of your publication
- it is in keeping with your publication's overall style
- it is wholly accurate in every respect
- it is legally safe to publish
- it is as easy and pleasant to read as possible.

Know how to knock it into shape

There will be some kind of shape already if the writer is competent, but the first thing to do is make sure that they have dealt with the correct subject in the manner asked for (this is the equivalent, to refer back to our opening joke, of knowing that you are in a balloon). It helps to have a good idea of what the commission was and how this piece is planned to fit into the issue as a whole. This will give you a firm basis on which to start making judgments about quality and appropriateness. You must also know the length that was commissioned because it is your job to make sure the piece has the required number of words.

Know your medium

It is possible, and increasingly likely, that your publication will take more than one form; it could be printed, it could be uploaded onto a website, it could be cannibalised for delivery to WAP or G3 mobile phones and it could also appear on television. Although there is no fully integrated model of this sort at the time of writing, there are many 'halfway houses': printed newspapers and magazines have associated web and WAP sites, and a number of magazines have so-called masthead television programmes extending their brands.

There are forms of subediting for all of them and it is important that you know how to present copy effectively for whichever medium you are working in. Reading habits differ across them, so you need to know whether to make copy short and punchy or whether you can let it stretch out. If there is a layout element to the job, you must be aware that what works beautifully across the double-page spread of an A4 glossy will not work in the same way on the typical 800 × 600 resolution of a computer screen. Mobile devices like phones and handheld computers are even more limiting.

Know your readers

This is perhaps the key rule for all subeditors. You need a very clear understanding of the readership of your publication and, most importantly, of how much they are likely to know about a subject. Only then can you make sensible decisions about clarifying or condensing copy. How much specialised jargon will they understand? Are the basic principles of a complex technical process clear enough for a general readership? Conversely, has the writer taken a 'Janet and John' approach when Stephen Hawking would have been a better model? The editor and the publisher should have the idealised reader engraved on their hearts, so ask them. Keep an eye on the letters page, too; it may give you an indication of how a particular piece was received.

Know your house style

The whys and wherefores of house style are dealt with in the next chapter. Suffice it to say here that having a firm grasp of your publication's preferences in matters of alternative spellings, usage and points of punctuation is essential for fast and accurate subediting. Those with responsibility for layout should also be completely familiar with the house rules on page furniture and the like.

Know your spelling and grammar

At the risk of sounding like a superannuated schools' inspector, a great many people will not have been taught how to spell or how to construct a sentence and might not even be aware of the importance of these elements in written communication. If this sounds like you (and nobody is blaming you here), do something about it. At the very least you need a big dictionary and a copy of a book like *English for Journalists* – and you need to use them both.

However, even people who have been through the mill of parsing sentences and spelling bees have blind spots when it comes to certain words. Acknowledge these entirely human weaknesses and use that dictionary whenever you are unsure of either the spelling or the meaning.

Know what you don't know

The same goes for general knowledge. Even if you are a champion Trivial Pursuit player there will be times when you are unsure of a fact. Do not assume that the writer is correct; do not assume that your 95 per cent certainty will suffice – look it up. For this you will need a good reference book (even better, a set of reference books) or an encyclopedia. Or . . .

Know how to search the internet effectively

Just about everything you ever need to know can be found somewhere on the internet. The trick is to find it quickly and to be sure that the information is correct. If you don't already know how to do this – and even if you do – consult a book such as *The Internet Handbook for Writers, Researchers and Journalists* by Mary McGuire *et al.* or Reddick and King's *The Online Journalist.*

Know why you are changing something

Despite what many writers pretend to believe, subeditors do not change copy for no reason, nor should they. Elementary corrections of spelling, grammar or factual error are easy to justify but it may be more difficult to explain why you altered the structure of a feature or rewrote a news story. If you find yourself thinking 'Why not change this?', turn the question around and ask 'Why change this?' It might save both time and heartache.

On the other hand, if you do change something for reasons which you believe to be sound and necessary, don't back down if the writer challenges you. The same applies to the writer of headlines, captions etc; a writer might not like the headline you put on their piece but if you did it in good faith and it helped to project or liven up their copy don't let even tears persuade you to change it.

Getting down to it

The guidelines above offer advice on how to regulate your job but they don't tell you how to get started. In fact, it's obvious – the first thing to do is read the copy. Look at it from the point of view of your readers, and trust your instincts – you're being paid to read it but if you find it boring, so will the reader.

The copy should, ideally, have been written by someone else, as subediting is essentially a matter of checking other people's work. However, in the real world of small staffs and editorial cutbacks it is increasingly common for writers to sub their own work (and on websites it seems to be standard practice). Subbing your own work is much more difficult than working on someone else's, making adherence to the following guidelines even more important.

Mark up or make a note of the things you need to check – dates, names, prices (especially if it's a consumer piece or you work on a contract or customer magazine), quotations, song titles. The latter can be surprisingly important for your self-esteem, as a sub working on the *Stage* weekly newspaper noted: 'Be mentally prepared to get zero credit for making absolute tripe copy come up smelling sweet, but much credit for knowing where the exclamation marks go in titles of Shania Twain songs.'

As the above quote suggests, note also where the copy needs to be tweaked up or rewritten but do bear in mind that guideline about having a good reason to change something. A sub working on a customer magazine for a major retail store came up with the following advice:

Subeditors across a wide range of publications, from national daily news-papers to quarterly magazines, were asked to list the most important lessons they have learnt over the years. These are the top five:

1   Unless you are 100 per cent sure, check. Assume nothing. Even the most reliable writers make mistakes.

2   Make space around you to print out a page and work on hard copy. Wear earplugs to help concentrate in a noisy office. Sub raw copy thoroughly; it's not a good idea to wait until it's on the page. Get as far ahead as you can; it's hard to sub in a rush.

3   Know your style guide/house style inside out.

4   Know your grammar and punctuation; if you weren't taught at school give yourself a crash course and buy a good book such as *English for Journalists*.

5   Know how to search the internet effectively.

Keep the original tone and voice of the writer; they have been asked to write that piece for a reason. Return to the author for advice if a piece has to be slashed to bits; sometimes asking them what has to stay in can speed everything up and keep everyone happy (well, happier, depending on the writer).

The same person suggests that regular liaison with the designers can help to keep the production process flowing smoothly. It certainly helps if you under-stand the pressures designers work under when it comes to choosing photo-graphs or graphics to accompany the copy, and also when adding the page furniture. This is the collective name for headlines, standfirsts, captions, cross-heads, pull quotes and all of the other typographical devices which add to the visual interest of the page (confusingly, some of these items have a number of names; see the glossary for explanations).

It is usually the subeditor's task to come up with the page furniture for a piece, and there are some very useful pieces of wisdom which have accrued over the years. First of all, this doesn't have to be a solo task (although the end product will always be your responsibility). Try bouncing ideas off colleagues; usually a little time spent trying to refine the idea is well spent. Refining and sharp-ening is almost always necessary in the case of standfirsts and, as for captions, a sub at Condé Nast was nearly right when he said: 'Smartarse photo captions

– smug and unfunny about 80 per cent of the time.' Nearly right because in truth it is more like 95 per cent.

A good way to avoid repeating words or ideas in headlines and standfirsts is to keep a list of those you have used already. When you're working on an issue with a particular theme, say spring, watch out that you don't end up over-doing 'fresh, light, bright' or fall into the 'ultimate guide to' kind of cliché.

When you are working on the various stages of an article or story, it can be difficult to keep all of these things in mind. Until you become practised in the art, and especially if you have to sub your own work, it is a good idea to keep a checklist and tick off each element as you do it.

Paul Dring, chief subeditor, *Food Illustrated*

My remit is: headlines; standfirsts; captions; blown quotes; fitting to length; ensuring the piece is well written – concise, to a good style, well-structured and with a good narrative flow; fact checking – names, spellings, titles, as well as assertions of fact themselves.

While this is my area of responsibility, it is not true to say that I alone provide a piece with heads, standfirsts, captions etc. This is very much a group effort and, often, the first caption or standfirst written is, in effect, a draft which is gradually revised to greater precision as more pairs of eyes look it over.

As regards subbing an individual piece, my basic raw material will be presented in one of two ways. The article will either be already laid out by a designer, or it will be in the form of raw copy from the contributor, not yet laid out. Either way, it will already be on the server: in the first case, a Quark document; in the second, Microsoft Word.

To begin subbing, I take a printout of the piece and read it through from start to finish, trying to maintain the same pace of reading as any first-time reader. After I've got an overall picture, I then make another printout on which I underline names and facts to be checked – my 'facts copy', which I tend to dip in and out of when I'm feeling least creative.

Before I start getting down to words and grammar, I have to content myself that the piece is correctly structured: do all the pars follow points set up in the previous par; are the linking sentences between pars strong enough; is there a clear narrative thread throughout the piece which addresses its central arguments?

Once I've decided that it is well-structured, I turn to the fine detail. My approach is often directed by how much overmatter is involved and how much space I've got to reclaim. To cut to fit, I first remove the excess verbiage and pay particular attention to pars which have, or nearly have, widows. I can usually cut a piece by a third in length before I have to start thinking about making a direct cut, and removing any of the sentences. Obviously though, if a sentence doesn't work, or is too much off at a tangent to the rest of the piece, I'll cut it regardless of the length of the piece. If I do have to cut any sentences, I bear in mind which pictures we're using, as the cut can become a caption. Fiddling with the tracking control is my last option, for single lines, and never to more than minus two.

Having said all this, though, I think one of the most important things is to be sensitive to the balance between brevity of expression and the writer's natural style – especially, for instance, in the case of columnists. After I've made my changes, it will be passed to other members of the editorial team, which usually results in some fine tuning. Normally about four other people cast their eyes over any feature, so really there's no excuse for any mistakes.

Will Ham Bevan, subeditor, *Daily Express*

The *Daily* and *Sunday Express* have a roster of 'casual' subeditors – freelances who work one or more evenings a week, and are paid by the shift. These are employed throughout the editorial departments, and I work on features.

When on duty, I report to that day's chief sub (DCS) or his deputy. As copy arrives, they will attach it to QuarkXPress layouts ('schemes' in newspaper parlance), and assign pages for me to work on.

The environment used – and fairly ubiquitous in newspapers, nowadays – is Quark Production System. The downtable subs like myself work in Quark Copy Desk, checking out individual bits of the page, such as body text, headlines and captions, to work on them. This allows more than one person to work on components of the same page, and also makes sure that the proof doesn't get corrupted – only the page sub, working in QuarkXPress, can change the actual geometry of the page.

When I first receive a story, I'll go through it and take out any extraneous returns – these often creep in when importing raw text. This will give me a rough idea of how long the copy is, and how much I'll need to cut. On the rare occasions when the copy is short, I'll alert the DCS to this, so that he can alter the geometry of the page or, if all else fails, chase up the writer for more copy.

I'll then edit the copy for grammar and house style, and make any obvious cuts. It's rare for me to have to make drastic alteration to the structure of the article, but I'll occasionally rejig an intro to make it stronger, or shuffle a few pars around to make the train of thought clearer. Nuts-and-bolts operations such as turning hyphens into em-dashes and single into double quotation marks are best tackled at this stage. Styling up the text comes next – putting in drop caps, crossheads, bullet points and the like. This done, I'll prune the copy to fit. Because page geometry can change very quickly on a newspaper (for instance, depending on advertisements) it's not unusual to have to take out a quarter to a third of all the words. Another consideration is the look of the copy across columns: the *Express* is fairly liberal about this, but orphans need to be taken out.

Once the text fits, I'll go into QPS and check out the headline, stand-first and captions. There are strict rules about writing display copy; nothing may be repeated in the furniture of the same page (such as a word appearing in both a headline and in a caption). I then spell-check everything, and check the page components back into the QPS database. At this point, I change their status from red ('editing') to amber ('for revise'). After this, one of the senior subs will give the piece a second reading, often making small alterations to a headline or caption, and will lock and pass the page as green ('for release') when they're satisfied with it.

Tim Holmes

3
House style

House style is the way a publication chooses to publish in matters of detail – single quotes or double, use of capitals and lower case, when to use italics, and so on. Putting a piece of copy into house style is the straightforward process of making it fit in with the rest of the publication. The main purpose is consistency rather than correctness.

The argument for consistency is very simple. Variation that has no purpose is distracting. By keeping a consistent style in matters of detail a publication encourages readers to concentrate on *what* its writers are saying.

House style, then, is for the benefit of the reader – and the writer – whereas style books, which codify house style, are primarily for the benefit of the sub. They exist to save time and trouble: to make it possible to apply a consistent style without wasting time checking in back issues or discussing all over again what was settled last week.

Ideally, staff writers and regular freelances make an effort to follow house style – but subs always have to check that they have done so. Copy supplied by agencies, occasional freelances and non-journalists, or contributed in the form of readers' letters, always needs the full treatment.

Some house-style decisions are both arbitrary and trivial. Whether a publication chooses tee-shirt or T-shirt, OK or okay, dreamt or dreamed, is not very important. It's hard to imagine anyone arguing passionately for one rather than another. But other decisions – foetus or fetus, for example – are clearly important since some readers consider one option 'correct' and the other 'incorrect'.

Style books go beyond consistency to rule on correctness in various ways. They include the correct spellings of commonly misspelt words (eg mantelpiece, minuscule, preventive), people's names (Gandhi, Mrs Beeton, Pete Townshend), company names (Harrods, PricewaterhouseCoopers, Marks & Spencer), places (Middlesbrough, Tunbridge Wells, Land's End) etc.

Also, they make recommendations about correct usage such as: don't use hopefully to mean it is hoped; do use chronic to mean recurrent rather than very bad; none must always be followed by a singular verb (but see Grammar/usage below). Since usage is often disputed – and constantly changing – and there is no *académie anglaise* to lay down the law about what is acceptable, style books do this job instead. Then writers and subs know what is expected of them by the editor or chief sub of their publication.

Of course this can work both ways: as well as insisting on what some people see as old-fashioned correctness, the style book can sanction a new/loose/colloquial usage as in '*authorities like Fowler and Gowers* is an acceptable alternative to *authorities such as Fowler and Gowers*' (*Economist*).

Style books lay down policy on swear words (when, if ever, to use them and whether to muffle them with asterisks), political correctness (eg don't use illegitimate for children born outside marriage, use actress of a female actor but not authoress of a female author, prefer hidden or parallel economy to black economy) and more general questions of style such as jargon, formal words and clichés. They can include reference lists (eg trade names, countries and their capitals, trade unions), typesetting instructions, proofreading signs, the main points of media law . . . a summary, in fact, of what the sub needs to know in order to work in a particular office.

Books on subbing have always covered the subject in some detail so it is curious that the latest edition of Harold Evans's famous guide to newspaper subbing *Newsman's English* (new title: *Essential English for Journalists, Editors and Writers*) has dropped its chapter on house style altogether – the term doesn't even appear in the index.

This is very much against the trend. House style is more widely covered than ever before. *ODWE* (*The Oxford Dictionary for Writers and Editors*, new edition 2000) advises on style, and so do various usage books.

An individual publication's house style is increasingly seen as an important part of its image and as a marketable commodity in its own right. Since 1986 when *The Economist Pocket Style Book* first appeared, Reuters (1992), the *Times* (1992, 1998) and the *Financial Times* (1994) have launched commercial editions of their in-house style books. The *Economist* has published six editions (the latest is called *The Economist Style Guide*), while the *Guardian*, as so often ahead of the game, has put its on its website where it is updated regularly.

These published style books promote their publications in two ways. First, they stress the publication's distinctive appeal ('The first requirement of *The Economist* is that it should be readily understandable'); second, they promise to help the reader write better – and not necessarily for the publication concerned (the guide is 'an invaluable companion for everyone who wants to communicate with the clarity, style and precision for which *The Economist* is renowned').

For example, the *Economist* proscribes the loose use of hopefully:

> **hopefully** By all means begin an article hopefully, but never write: *Hopefully, it will be finished by Wednesday.* Try: *With luck, if all goes well, it is hoped that* . . .

Other style books discouraging the loose use of hopefully are those of Reuters, the *Times*, the *Financial Times* and the *Observer* – whereas the *Guardian* wittily says:

> **hopefully** Sadly, this battle has been lost and hopefully is now widely used to mean it is to be hoped; mercifully, this is not the end of the world although it seems to upset the pedantic . . .

On other points, eg like/such as, where the *Economist* is prepared to give way (see above), the *Guardian* stands firm and refuses to give an inch. Its style book says:

> **like/such as** Like excludes; such as includes: 'Cities like Manchester are wonderful' suggests the writer has in mind, say, Sheffield or Birmingham; she actually means 'cities such as Manchester'.

This shows two important things. First, there is no consensus – even in the broadsheet press – on a number of these contentious points. Second, style evolves: it does not stand still. What the *Times* and the *Economist* ban today, they may approve tomorrow.

There are unmistakable trends in house style: in grammar, loose, colloquial usage is more accepted than it was; there is less punctuation, ie there are fewer capital letters, full stops for abbreviations, apostrophes, accents etc; in spelling, shorter forms are increasingly common and the American (and traditional English) -ize ending has lost ground to -ise, with the *Times* finally joining the rest of the press in the -ise camp.

There are various problems in applying house style. One is that a rule that works well in common examples may be harder to apply to less common ones. It's easy enough to say that wine from Bordeaux should be called bordeaux and brandy from Cognac should be called cognac, but what about the product of a more obscure place – Buzet, say, or Rouilly? Readers of a specialist magazine like *Decanter* may take buzet and rouilly in their stride but these lower-case wine names pose more of a problem for many newspaper readers.

Another problem is that, as newspapers publish more magazines and supplements aimed at specific groups of readers, it becomes progressively more difficult to apply a consistent style to them all. Interviews with rock stars, confessional columns and diaries should obviously have a looser style than news stories. And many style books, while saying that the grammar of direct quotes should often be corrected, stress that they should not be subject to the same rigorous streamlining treatment as copy in general.

Most style books are essentially an alphabetical list rather than a series of sections covering different subjects. This makes them easier to use and more effective. You might look up champagne to check that it's lower case and be reminded that the word can only be used of wine from Champagne (there is no such thing as 'Spanish champagne' and even 'champagne method' should no longer be used to describe other sparkling wines).

Before looking at a sample style book (see Appendix 1) it's worth considering some of the points usually covered under the obvious headings: spelling, punctuation, grammar etc.

Spelling

A style book should decide on the following two general questions:

1   -ise or -ize in words like realise and organize?
2   -t or -ed in words like spelt and learned?

As was noted above, the -ize spelling has virtually disappeared from British newspapers and magazines, though ODWE continues to recommend it. Spelt is preferred to spelled by the Times, the Observer, the Economist and the Financial Times but not by the Guardian; ODWE says use either. There are two arguments in favour of -t: that it is one character shorter and that learnt (gained knowledge) can be distinguished from learned (scholarly).

Another general question is whether to include the e in words like ageing, judgement, acknowledgement, likeable, loveable, fogey. But here there is no general answer: individual decisions must be made. Many would argue in favour of the shorter form unless it looks wrong – hence judgment but ageing.

With some pairs of words including or dropping the e can clarify the distinction between them:

linage (payment by the line)/lineage (descent)
dying (the death)/dyeing (clothes)
singing (a song)/singeing (burning)

swinging (London)/swingeing (heavy)
holy (grail)/holey (jumper).

Other examples of spelling distinctions that reflect meaning, are:

bogy (ghost)/bogey (in golf)/bogie (undercarriage)
pedaller (cyclist)/peddler (drug dealer)/pedlar (hawker)
bale out (of aircraft)/bail out (boat, prisoner, company).

Not recommended in general is the attempt to use two different spellings of the same word to convey (sometimes slight) differences in meaning eg:

far/farther/farthest (of distance) but far/further/furthest (of everything else)
judgement (personal opinion) but judgment (legal ruling)
enquiry (informal question) but inquiry (official investigation).

The *Guardian* and the *Economist* make the first of these distinctions; *ODWE* the last two. All three are obsolete, if they were ever in general use, and it is perverse to continue to make them. But there are two such distinctions in general use:

disk (in computing) but disc (in everything else)
program (in computing) but programme (in everything else).

(Computing also provides us with the aberrant spellings format/formatted/formatting – compare with combat/combated/combating.)

Other oddities include movable (the preferred spelling – but Hemingway's memoirs were called 'A Moveable Feast' and the e spelling is used in legal documents) and elder/eldest (alternatives to older/oldest mainly used in family relationships).

Words like encyclopaedia and mediaeval, which can lose their middle a, have done so almost everywhere: the ae diphthong now looks archaic. But there is resistance in some quarters to foetus losing its o on the grounds that fetus is 'American'. In fact the word comes from the Latin *fetus*, offspring, so there is a strong case for the shorter form. *ODWE* and the *Economist* prefer fetus, which is now gradually gaining acceptance.

The plurals of words ending in o can present problems. Most of them (hero, potato, veto) take es in the plural, but some (banjo, halo, salvo) take either s or es: in these cases the style book should give clear guidance.

What about words of recognisably foreign origin, whether Latin, Greek, French, Italian or whatever? In the plural should they be virtuosi or virtuosos, memoranda or memorandums, châteaux (with the accent) or chateaus? In some cases distinctions can be drawn: between media (the press etc) and mediums (spiritualists); appendices (of books) and appendixes (of the body); bureaux de change (for money) and bureaus (furniture). Again the style book should be clear.

Another word of foreign origin that causes trouble is blond and its feminine form blonde. Whereas women are obviously blonde(s), their hair colour (not being feminine) should remain blond. French has a similar problem with the English word sandwich: le sandwich and therefore in the plural les sandwichs; but in imitation of the English plural this often becomes les sandwiches.

Punctuation

Punctuation shows the biggest changes in house style. In almost every case there is less punctuation now than there was. Exceptions are full stops between sentences – because sentences are shorter there are now more full stops – and paragraph breaks. In every other case there is less punctuation.

Full stops to mark abbreviations and contractions have virtually disappeared, while in page furniture – headlines, standfirsts, captions etc – the final full stop is rare.

Back in the 18th century when newspapers started publishing they scattered caps about like confetti. An early cricket report read: 'The game ended to a very great Nicety in favour of the Kentish Gentlemen, but had so many diverting Turns in it, that the Lovers of that Diversion esteem it to be the best that has been played for many years.'

Until recently many newspapers still used caps for the Press, the Law, the Government, and so on. But nowadays you have a lower-case chancellor of the exchequer, stock exchange and financial services authority. In the *Guardian* only the City (of London) keeps its initial cap – the church (of England) and the internet have lost theirs.

Apostrophes are far less common than they were. In 1930 a former editor of the *Daily Express*, Ralph Blumenfeld, produced a style book for the paper called 'Do's and Don't's for Reporters and Sub-Editors' – note the three apostrophes. By 1968 when Leslie Sellers, production editor of the *Daily Mail*, published *Doing it in Style*, there were only two: do's and don'ts. And in its 2000 edition *ODWE* recommended just one: dos and don'ts.

John o'Groat's has been a victim of this trend. This was originally John o'Groat's House (the house of a Dutchman called John who came from Groat) but as the house fell down or was forgotten the second apostrophe tended to get lost. Both the *Times* and *ODWE* say it should be used – to stop poor John being associated with a non-existent place called Groats.

The phrase p's and q's still needs apostrophes if it's lower case, whereas in caps Ps and Qs works perfectly well. This illustrates an important pragmatic point: apostrophes are used where necessary to make meaning clearer; where they are not necessary, they can be – should be – left out.

The same goes for hyphens. There is never a reason for adding a hyphen to an -ly adverb: 'closely-knit' is a ridiculous usage because closely used before knit can only mean 'knit in a close way'. By contrast 'close-knit' may need a hyphen to confirm that close refers to knit.

Failure to use hyphens properly can have hilarious results. In April 2000 an Oxford professor admonished the *Times* for appearing to condone cruelty to animals by merely noting that 'hot dog-munching sports fans' were filling American baseball parks. Similar fun can be had with 'extra marital sex' (married couples working overtime instead of committing adultery) and 'light housekeepers' instead of 'lighthouse-keepers'.

More seriously, the *Guardian* once had to publish a letter complaining that the account of a rape highlighted the perpetrator's skin colour (black cab-driver) where the writer had intended to refer to the driver of a London licensed taxi (black-cab driver). The *Guardian* now includes this illustration in its style book.

In general it gives the sound advice that, where possible, commonly hyphenated words should drop the hyphen to make a single word – birthplace, email, headteacher, passerby, subeditor, swearword, theatregoer, uncooperative, wicketkeeper are some examples of this policy.

Grammar/usage

These points are taken together because they are almost impossible to separate and people constantly confuse them. All sorts of usage preferences are mistakenly called 'grammatical' rather than stylistic.

For example, splitting infinitives may be bad style but it is not bad grammar. Nor is ending a sentence with a preposition, or starting one with a conjunction. And nor is following the word none with a plural verb. The *Economist* mildly observes that none 'usually takes a singular verb'; the *Times* goes an unwise step further: 'none almost always takes the singular verb'. But it is left to the *Guardian* to close the door: 'none takes singular verb: none is, not none are.'

Which is nonsense. As Bill Bryson (once deputy chief sub on the *Times*) memorably wrote in 1984: 'The widely held belief that none must always be singular is a myth ... Fowler, Bernstein, Howard, Gowers, Partridge, the Evanses, the Morrises, Follett, *The Oxford English Dictionary*, *The American Heritage*, *Random House* and *Webster's New World* dictionaries and many others have already made this point.'

Leslie Sellers in 1968 gave the following simple guidance: 'None can be either singular or plural, depending on the way it is used. Use a singular verb when it means "no quantity" and "not one"; use a plural verb when it means "not any" and when it means "no people" or "no things".' And *ODWE* (2000) is simpler still: 'None can be followed by singular or plural verb according to the sense.'

Similar to the ban on plural verbs after none is the ruling that companies and other organisations must take a singular verb. Whereas the none ban is ignorant, the companies ruling is a legitimate house-style decision. But it certainly creates practical problems in writing stories about them since we often think of them as plural entities.

Prepositions cause all sorts of apparent problems: bored *by/with* or *of*; centre *in/on* or *around*; compare *to* or *with*; different *from* or *to* or *than*; fed up *with* or *of*; try *to* or *and*? Some of these questions are easy to answer: bored and fed up *of* belong with 'Sorted' and 'Cheers, mate' in the mockney dialect; try *and* is more colloquial than try *to* but hardly noticeable; centre *around* is self-contradictory; compare *to* and *with* are different and the difference is useful.

But the word different poses a real problem: style books traditionally prescribe different *from* – it's preferable on logical grounds – but millions of otherwise literate people now write different *to*. At least one style book has bitten the bullet: the *Financial Times* prefers different *from* but says 'there is nothing grammatically wrong with the phrase *different to*'. It adds: '*Different than* is common in the US; it should be resisted.' So the *FT* sub is recommended to write different *from*, licensed to leave different *to* and instructed to change different *than*.

A similar policy could be adopted over the use of *that* and *which* in relative clauses, a traditional distinction still made in most style books but in practice widely disregarded by British writers. In her book *Verbal Hygiene* English professor Deborah Cameron tells an instructive tale about the editing stage of an American encyclopedia in which some British contributors refused to accept their copy editors' changes of *which* to *that*. The compromise 'solution' was to publish the book with the American *whiches* and *thats* put into house style but the British ones all over the place. Which rather defeats the object of the exercise – consistency.

If the *which/that* distinction is on the way out, though still useful, why not continue to recommend it but license the failure to make it – unless there is genuine obscurity? *Like/such as* is going this way (see above). Then there is the position of only (which would justify 'I'm only here for the beer'), the use of due to mean because of, and so on.

Words

Words often mean different things to different people. One function of a style book is to specify how a particular word is to be used: is disinterested, for example, to be used to mean impartial (the original, educated, 'correct' usage) or bored – another way of saying uninterested (the loose, colloquial, 'incorrect' usage)? Is celibate to mean unmarried or abstaining from sex? Decimate to mean kill one in 10 or massacre? Chauvinist to mean flag-waver or sexist?

Style books need to decide which of two usages is preferred, or whether the context should determine the issue, or whether the word is more trouble than it's worth – because of the confusion it creates – so shouldn't be used at all. Decimate, fulsome and inchoate probably come into this last category. Verbal, on the other hand, can mean both related to words and spoken: a verbal agreement is spoken, verbal reasoning is not – both are clear.

The style book for a medical magazine may well say that chronic is to be used of recurrent illnesses, not very bad ones. The style book for *Police Review* should remind its journalists that an alibi is not any old excuse but a plea that when an alleged act took place the suspect was elsewhere. The style book for a chess magazine will probably not need to remind contributors that a gambit is always an opening. But outside these specialist areas the words chronic, alibi and gambit are more likely to be used loosely; the style book should say whether this matters.

The word refute should be included in every style book because it is now used by many people to mean deny whereas it has traditionally meant disprove. The style books and experts are unanimous in endorsing the traditional – and criticising the loose, colloquial – usage. But in doing so they often create a further problem.

For they disagree about the word rebut and how it relates to refute. Two of them (the *Economist* and the *FT*) say that it means much the same as refute: 'rebut and refute mean to put to flight or disprove in argument' (*Economist*). Two of them (the *Observer* and the *Guardian*) say the opposite: 'refute is not a synonym for deny or rebut' (*Observer*). And two more say something completely different.

The *Times* says that 'rebut means to argue to the contrary, producing evidence; refute is to win such an argument' while Bill Bryson comes up with an entirely new idea. 'Refute,' he says, 'means to show that an allegation is wrong. Rebut means to disprove an allegation and answer in kind.'

The commonsense solution here is to put both words on the banned list – refute because it is often used and is often confusing, rebut because it is rarely used but on the evidence above is always confusing.

Foreign words pose several problems: should they be widely used, should they be italicised, should they keep their accents? In general, should they be used accurately, as in the original language, or can they mean anything at all? Two vogue words in British journalism are actualité to mean truth (as in 'economical with the actualité') and embonpoint to mean ample bosom, then by extension cleavage. Both these usages are given in *The Oxford Dictionary of Foreign Words and Phrases*. But *ODWE* by sticking to French is a better guide: for actualité it gives present state, for embonpoint, plumpness.

American words keep coming into British usage. Our children are raised now more often than brought up, and they play with toy trucks more often than lorries. But a pay increase is still a rise, not a raise; and a hike is still a walk across country, not a rise.

Some contrasts in usage are charming and should be kept. Londoners can surely live with Smollensky's *on* the Strand almost next door to Simpson's *in* the Strand – one is an American jazz joint, the other an old-fashioned English restaurant. But Americans who write envision can expect it to become envisage, just as center becomes centre.

Seafood is a useful word if it means 'fish and shellfish taken together' but a pointless alternative to 'shellfish' by itself. Indeed worse than pointless: a piece on the health benefits of oily fish and shellfish rather than white fish was not helped by the appearance of the word seafood somewhere in the middle. Meaning, as always, is the crux.

Names

The names of people and places should be listed in the style book if people often get them wrong or there is disagreement about them. Jeane has often been spelt that way in the United States, eg by Marilyn Monroe (Norma Jeane) and the UN ambassador Jeane Kirkpatrick; Vinnie Jones is not Vinny; Marianne Faithfull has two ll's; the ancient British queen Boadicea has become Boudicca; Thomas à Becket has lost the à and is plain Becket nowadays. Roumania now prefers to be Romania and Peking is Beijing.

The British have always called Firenze Florence and Milano Milan and added an s to Lyon and Marseille. But the *Guardian* style book has surely started a trend by doing away with the s.

Clichés

All style books discourage clichés; some list the ones they particularly dislike, eg a catch-22 situation, to die for, ironically, 'share a joke' (in captions), wryly (to signal a joke) . . . Even worse than any of these are clichés used wrongly: playing King Canute, for example, to mean stupidly resisting progress; begging the question for raising the question; the curate's egg for something part good, part bad; Hobson's choice for a difficult choice; Frankenstein for a monster . . . These should be banned because they are stale, confusing and intensely irritating to some people.

Policy questions

Many style books include a general statement on such things as the editing of quotes (see pp. 60–1) and swear words. The *Times* says: 'Four-letter words and profanities should be avoided. However, in direct quotes and where they are essential to the story, style obscenities with asterisks: f***, c*** etc.'

On this last point the *Guardian* says the opposite: 'Never use asterisks, which are just a copout.'

As well as admitting that it uses more swear words than any other paper, the *Guardian* is in the vanguard when it comes to political correctness (although it discourages the term as a cliché), for example:

black economy
prefer hidden or parallel economy

disabled people
not 'the disabled'. Use positive language about disability, avoiding outdated terms that stereotype or stigmatise . . .

gender issues
Our use of language should reflect not only changes in society but the newspaper's values. Phrases such as career girl or career woman, for example, are outdated (more women have careers than men) and patronising (there is no male equivalent): never use them.

Gypsy (not gypsy)

racial terminology
Do not use 'ethnic' to mean black or Asian people . . .

But the *Guardian* is less keen to humour Catholics:

Catholic
does not always mean Roman Catholic. If Roman Catholic is meant, say so at first mention

Londonderry
not Derry, except where Derry is part of the name of an institution or organisation . . .

Whether you agree with these points or not they are an excellent example of house style – of a newspaper's use of language reflecting its values.

For a sample style book see Appendix 1 on p. 155.

Wynford Hicks

4
Correcting mistakes

You could fill a book with examples of bad English taken from newspapers and magazines. Indeed Harry Blamires, a retired English teacher and literary critic, claims to do this in *Correcting your English* (Bloomsbury 1996), though some of his rulings are a bit pedantic and in places he is himself mistaken. (For example, he says that 'none' must be followed by a singular verb – see House style, pp. 25–6.)

Below are examples of some of the common mistakes that subs should learn to spot and correct.

Hanging participles . . .

A participle ('following', 'having followed') must have the same subject as the main verb in a sentence; otherwise it is said to be hanging or dangling.

Here's the start of the second par of a broadsheet cricket report: 'Following on 188 runs behind England after being bowled out for 203 in their first innings – in a reduced match the follow-on is also reduced from 200 to 150 – there were fewer than four scheduled overs of the day remaining when the Pakistan captain Waqar Younis was caught at the wicket to concede defeat.'

The par goes on: 'Bowled out second time around for 179, the majority of the wickets came . . .' And the next one reads: 'Backed by some outstanding close catching, particularly from Graham Thorpe, the first innings honours went to Gough . . .'

Once is bad enough – but three times in close succession? This writer's problem is trying to say too much in a single sentence, so in rewriting, simplify:

'Pakistan, who made 203 in their first innings, followed on 188 runs behind England (in a reduced match the follow-on is 150) and were bowled out for 179 with just four overs of the day's play left. Most of the wickets came . . .'

Some writers seem to find it difficult to start a sentence without a hanging participle: 'Having become Lord Chancellor, Maxwell Fyfe's political career ended in 1962 when he was sacked from the Cabinet in the "Night of the Long Knives". Complaining to Macmillan that he had been given less notice than was needed to dismiss a cook, Macmillan replied that it was more difficult to get a good cook than a Lord Chancellor.'

Without much effort this becomes: 'Maxwell Fyfe lost his job as Lord Chancellor in 1962 in the Night of the Long Knives. When he complained that he had been given less notice than was needed to dismiss a cook, Macmillan replied that a good cook was more difficult to find than a Lord Chancellor.'

Instructional copy is full of hanging participles: 'Once plugged in, the instructions are easy to follow.'

Rewrite this simply as: 'Plug in the appliance and the instructions are easy to follow.'

Obituaries and brief biographies are similarly afflicted: 'Born in Ilford, her father worked at Ford's Dagenham factory.'/'Born in Geraldton, Gallop and Blair forged a close friendship at Oxford University.'

The problem comes from over-compression. Rewrite as: 'She was born in Ilford; her father worked at Ford's Dagenham factory.'/'Gallop, who was born in Geraldton, and Blair became close friends at Oxford University.'

The malady sometimes seems universal: 'Arriving in Bournemouth determined to be fair it was an impossible task.'/'Once diagnosed as terminal, when there was "nothing more the hospital could do", it was suggested my mother enter a hospice.'/'Being summer, I half expected him to reply . . .'

But the cure is not difficult: 'Arriving in Bournemouth determined to be fair I found the task impossible.'/'Once my mother was diagnosed as terminal . . . it was suggested she enter a hospice.'/'Because it was summer I half expected him to reply . . .'

. . . and other dangling modifiers

'Like' and 'as' trap many writers: 'Like many excluded children, the school labelled Nathan a bully.'/'Like Ian Katz nothing prepared me for the shock of the settlements.'

Rewrite straightforwardly as: 'Like many excluded children, Nathan was labelled a bully by the school.'/'Like Ian Katz I was completely unprepared for the shock of the settlements.'

'As a teenager, they drank frozen daiquiris together.'/'As a reader acquainted with more than one might care to know about Millet's appetites and anatomy, the prospect of lunch with the author was disconcerting.'

The first is easy enough to deal with – if you know the rest of the story. Rewrite as: 'When Hemingway's son Jack was a teenager, they drank frozen daiquiris together.'

The second is something else: it's written by an English male journalist embarrassed by the thought of meeting a scandalously sexy French woman writer and trying to distance himself – as well as its dangling modifier, the sentence has variation (eg 'the author' for Millet, see below) and all sorts of other pomposities (eg 'anatomy' for body). But a total rewrite here risks losing the tone of the piece (however much you may dislike it) – it's safer to restrict yourself to essential tidying up: 'As a reader knowing more than one might care to know about Millet's appetites and anatomy, I was disconcerted by the prospect of having lunch with her.'

Sometimes the dangling modifier goes beyond clumsiness and creates confusion: 'Blake used a homemade ladder to scale the prison walls, and Pottle and Randle smuggled him away. After a few months lying low at Pottle's Hampstead flat, Randle drove Blake to East Berlin.'

As you read it the piece seems to say that it is Randle who has been lying low at Pottle's flat. But this is nonsense: Blake not Randle is the escaped prisoner. Rewrite as: 'Blake spent a few months lying low at Pottle's flat; then Randle drove him to East Berlin.'

Active and passive

Editors and trainers often tell trainee reporters: where possible use active rather than passive verbs. Write 'Firefighters rescued the man', rather than 'The man was rescued by firefighters', because it is more direct and vivid.

But as a sub you have to be able to use both the active and the passive and to convert one to the other. In the example above, 'Like many excluded children, the school labelled Nathan a bully', the problem is in the conflict between the modifier ('Like many excluded children') and the subject of the sentence ('the school'). The simplest rewrite is to keep the modifier and follow it by the correct subject ('Nathan'), then change the active verb ('the school labelled') to the passive ('was labelled by the school'): 'Like many excluded children, Nathan was labelled a bully by the school.'

Repetition . . .

Repetition for effect is an important rhetorical device. But sometimes it is unintentional and inept: 'Unless the Tories can counter the threat from the Lib Dems, the Tories will face many more years in the wilderness.'

The writer seems to have avoided 'they' for 'the Tories' second time round to avoid confusion with the Lib Dems – but why not use 'they' first time round? 'Unless they can counter the threat from the Lib Dems, the Tories will face many more years in the wilderness.'

. . . and variation

It's always dangerous to rename a spade a 'gardening tool' in an attempt to avoid repetition or add colour to copy. The reporter (or sub) who put the phrase 'Alpine country' in the intro below made it ludicrous:

'Government negotiations with Austria's far-right Freedom party were continuing in Vienna last night in the face of controversial threats by all other European Union governments to isolate the Alpine country.'

This is ludicrous because the geography of Austria has no bearing on the story: there's no connection between mountains and far-right politics. It's almost as naff as calling the Netherlands 'the land of tulips' or Switzerland 'the land of chocolates' in stories about war criminals.

At least cut 'Alpine'. Or rewrite as follows: 'The Austrian government was continuing negotiations with the far-right Freedom party last night in the face of controversial threats by all other European Union governments to isolate Austria.'

The phrase 'Jewish state' is used in the next example to avoid a third 'Israel/ Israeli': 'Hours later Israeli tanks shelled the home of a Palestinian security chief who has frequently taken part in peace negotiations with the Jewish state, in an attack bound to sharpen criticism of Israel's use of inappropriate measures to snuff out the Palestinian intifada.'

The problem here is caused by the reporter's insistence on dotting every i. Cut some of the countries and the par is still clear: 'Hours later Israeli tanks shelled the home of a Palestinian security chief who has often taken part in peace negotiations. The attack is bound to sharpen criticism of Israel's use of inappropriate measures to snuff out the intifada.'

The variation can be apparently relevant – but still awkward: 'But then Afghanistan is in the grip of a revolution of its own. In the Islamic state women are forbidden to work; men are punished for not growing beards . . .'

Either cut 'In the Islamic state' (because readers don't need to be reminded) or change it to something like 'under Islamic rule'.

Some writers seem to take a perverse delight in thinking up synonyms and alternatives: you get variation on variation. In the following example whatever happened to 'South Africa'? 'One of the apartheid state's most notorious assassins has for the first time linked the former white regime's security forces to a massacre that almost wrecked negotiations to end minority rule.'

Rewrite as: 'One of South Africa's most notorious assassins has for the first time linked the former regime's security forces to a massacre that almost wrecked negotiations to end apartheid.'

Variation can be ludicrous: 'Dropping charges for children in April 1999 resulted in a 20 per cent increase in child visitors. The next phase saw pensioners getting in free from April 2000 and resulted in a 40 per cent increase in visits by senior citizens.'

Rewrite as: 'Dropping charges for children in April 1999 resulted in a 20 per cent increase in child visits; dropping them for pensioners in April 2000 resulted in a 40 per cent increase in pensioner visits.'

Variation can be misleading: 'Robert Mochrie, a 49-year-old property owner, was found hanging on the landing of his five bedroom home in a suburb of Barry, Vale of Glamorgan, after police officers forced their way into the property on Sunday evening.'

The phrase 'property owner' does not mean that Mochrie owned his own home but that property owning was his business – using 'the property' as a variation on 'his home' is crass. Replace 'into the property' by 'in'.

And here's a *Guardian* correction that shows how some people are misled:

> In a report headed 'New *Express* owners set the tone with Beckhams' visit', page 7, November 29, we attributed a quoted remark to 'one veteran at the in-house newsletter, Crusader'. Our media correspondent had simply used the term 'the Crusader', meaning the paper itself, the *Daily Express*, and was referring to the crusader device in its masthead. He had no idea that it had an in-house newsletter called the Crusader (a reference inserted in the editing) and that is not where his quote came from.
> (*Guardian* Corrections and clarifications 2 December 2000)

The unwary sub had not spotted that the media correspondent was indulging in variation ('the Crusader' for the *Express*), assumed that the phrase meant something and changed the copy accordingly. The moral is clear: always be on the lookout for variation.

Misused clichés

Poor old King Canute. Of all the clichés misused daily by newspapers and magazines 'playing King Canute' to mean being overtaken by unforeseen disaster or resisting change is the most idiotic. According to the traditional anecdote, Canute (or Cnut) went down to the seashore to show his courtiers that the waves would not obey him – that he was not in fact omnipotent. So King Canute can't be invoked to ridicule local people who object to change.

'Frinton Canutes face tide of alcohol' (about opposition to a proposed pub) is a typical example of this nonsense.

Another misused cliché is 'proving the rule'. This cannot logically mean that an exception to a rule helps make it valid. Yet that nonsensical meaning is assumed here: 'Over the past couple of decades, few on-stage duos have made any kind of impression – French and Saunders and Reeves and Mortimer are the exceptions that prove the rule.'

All this means is that French and Saunders and Reeves and Mortimer are exceptions to the generalisation (clearly not a rule) that there haven't been many successful duos recently. Correct as follows: 'Over the past couple of decades, few on-stage duos have made any kind of impression – except French and Saunders and Reeves and Mortimer.'

Here's another example: 'Coalition governments have been rare since the mid-19th century (which is to say since the birth of organised mass parties), with the rule-proving exceptions of wartime coalitions of national unity.'

This is another generalisation, not a rule (see the word 'rare'); and it cannot be 'proved' by exceptions. Correct by deleting 'rule-proving'.

Begging the question (like 'the exception proves the rule') has a technical meaning but nowadays is usually used to mean 'raising the question': 'Callaway's answer, "Go buy an ERC2", was received with loud laughter, but with the club priced at $625 (about £430), obviously begged a question.'

Correct by replacing 'begged' by 'raised'.

'Begging the question' is now spawning variants as here: 'The very fact that there was a camera crew inside No 10 rather begged the conclusion that in fact he had hired a lemon.'

Correct as follows (also cutting the repetitive 'in fact'): 'The very fact that there was a camera crew inside No 10 suggested he had hired a lemon.'

Then there are those misused clichés that are just mistakes, mishearings, mismatches, whatever: 'It's as clear as a pikestaff that they are deliberately trying to undermine the government's efforts.'

This should be 'as plain as a pikestaff'. Without the familiar alliteration the phrase sounds ridiculous: how can a pikestaff be clear? (According to Brewer the phrase was originally 'plain as a packstaff' – the staff on which a pedlar carried his pack, worn plain and smooth.)

Pronoun confusion

Pronouns must be clear. In the following example who/what does 'their' in the last line refer to? The stars, the readers, the tabloids, the proprietors, the editors?

'Successful editors and proprietors know the sad truth, that bitchery is a necessary ingredient of the tabloids. Millions of readers enjoy regular doses of *Schadenfreude* when stars are cut down to size even while slapping their wrists.'

The sense of the par is that tabloid editors and proprietors are mildly disapproved of by their readers who nevertheless enjoy what they produce. Here check with the writer (a specialist media correspondent) pointing out that readers are hardly in a position to do much wrist-slapping.

In the next example who does the last 'they' refer to? The voters or their MPs?

'The Goldsmith-backed Democracy Movement will start this week to distribute more than 2m pamphlets resembling local newspapers. They will tell voters not to support their MPs if they want to keep the pound.'

The sense of the par is that keeping the pound is the priority of both the Democracy Movement and some voters but not of the MPs mentioned. Rewrite the second sentence as: 'They will tell voters who want to keep the pound not to support their MPs.'

In the following example 'we' suddenly changes from its first meaning, 'Asian or black', to include everyone who watches television – 'We see more black and brown faces than we used to . . .'

'Most Asian or black people, particularly the young, have a wide range of friends. Most of us work in settings that are predominantly white, and few of us are culturally separate from those around us. We see more black and brown faces than we used to; but it's a slow uphill grind . . .'

Rewrite the last sentence as: 'There are more black and brown faces on TV than there used to be . . .'

Misused prepositions

Prepositions are often misused as here: 'The woman who has become a cult figure to millions of sci-fi devotees as FBI special agent Dana Scully plays a New York society beauty at the turn of the century, torn between marrying for status or for love.'

'Between' must be followed by 'and' so rewrite the ending as: 'torn between marrying for status and marrying for love'.

Should it be different to, from or than? The following example shows why 'to' can cause problems: 'Do women behave differently to men in war zones?'

Does this mean 'behave differently towards men' or 'behave differently from men'? On the assumption that it means 'from men' use this formula – which is clear and correct.

In the next example 'than' should be replaced by 'from': 'It would have seemed no different than putting one's name on top of a bit of ghost-written garbage in a newspaper.'

Another mismatch is 'identical . . . as' (it should be 'identical to'/'the same as') as here: 'He pointed out that comprehensive-educated students got an identical proportion of first class degrees as former independent school pupils last summer despite getting slightly worse A levels on average.'

Rewrite as: 'He pointed out that comprehensive-educated students got the same proportion of first class degrees as those who had gone to independent schools . . .'

'Bored' and 'fed up' take 'with' not 'of': 'I have been single since Christmas and I'm bored of spending the weekends with married friends.'/'Everyone's fed up of ball breakers, aren't they?'

Change 'of' to 'with' in both cases.

Clumsy construction

'England's task is to at least come away with a draw from Manchester.'

This is a badly split infinitive: 'at least', which splits the infinitive 'to come away', is in the wrong place for the sense of the sentence and any kind of rhythm. Rewrite as: 'England's task is to come away from Manchester with at least a draw.'

'For such a prime minister, parliamentary debate, while not an important inconvenience, has nothing to tell him.'

The sentence is made up of two parts that do not fit together: if it starts with 'for such a prime minister' it can't end with 'has nothing to tell him'. Rewrite as: 'For such a prime minister, parliamentary debate . . . has nothing to say.'

'Sales of wine to drink at home rose by 15 per cent in the first quarter of 2001 compared to the same quarter in 2000.'

The construction distorts the meaning: wine sales didn't (necessarily) rise by 15 per cent over the course of the first quarter of 2001: at that point in the year they were 15 per cent higher than they had been. Rewrite as: 'Sales of wine to drink at home were 15 per cent higher in the first quarter of 2001 than in the same quarter in 2000.'

'Teacher salaries in England compared favourably with other countries.'

No, they didn't: they compared favourably with those in other countries. Insert 'those in' after 'with'.

Wrong verb

Using the simple present tense where the subjunctive is needed can be very misleading: 'The key, says Dr McDonnell of the Catholic Communications Centre, is that "the culture of broadcasting is not lost" in the new age.'

Change 'is not' to 'should not be', removing the double quote marks.

'Seamus Hegarty lambasts Chris Woodhead for suggesting Ofsted is the agent for educational research.'

Change 'is' to 'should be'.

'A prudish word in Charlie's ear suggested she wears a bra.'

Change 'wears' to 'should wear'.

The most common example of this mistake is the failure to distinguish between 'may' and 'might': 'Hill may have made it less of a mountain.'

This headline is contradicted by the copy underneath which says: 'If any one player can make a difference, it is tempting to say that Hill might have done at Stadium Australia on Saturday.'

Change 'may' to 'might'.

Singular v plural

Mixing up singular and plural is easily done: 'People who've never won trophies, raffles, egg-and-spoon races and how-much-does-the-cake-weigh competitions – they are the sort who phones up to win nothing.'

Change 'phones' to 'phone'.

'A certain amount of international politics are almost inevitable in seeking a successor to Richards.'

Change 'are' to 'is'.

Sometimes a parenthesis helps to create confusion: 'The nature of the tests, which were carried out by the Queen's physician, are confidential.'/'The condition of many barracks and married quarters are rapidly deteriorating.'/'He has left behind a glorious body of work – seven novels and two non-fiction books – which are treasured by his tens of millions of fans.'

In all cases change 'are' to 'is'.

In some countries (though not Britain) newspapers insist on treating sports teams as singular: 'India ended the second day in Madras on 211 for one in its first innings after the tourists folded from 340 for three to 391 all out.'

The 'its' here contrasts strangely with the plural 'tourists'.

And as the next example (from the same paper) shows, the singular is difficult to sustain: 'South Africa, 56 runs behind West Indies on first innings, was 43 for two in their second innings at tea Monday, on the third day of the second test in Port of Spain, Trinidad.'

Singular or plural is a matter of house style: follow it. But 'was 43 for two in their second innings' is bad grammar: correct it.

Redundancy

'Both chancellor and prime minister delivered a brace of fine speeches, passionate and substantial.'

'Both Labour and the Tories have shared a fundamental misapprehension for much of the past century.'

Both these sentences look as though they suffer from the problem of redundancy – saying the same thing twice. In the second example there is no doubt: either 'both' or 'shared' is redundant; to solve the problem and keep the writer's style, cut 'both'.

But in the first example it's just possible that the sentence means what it says: the chancellor made two fine speeches, and so did the prime minister – four fine speeches in all. This is a reminder of the important, if obvious, point that bad grammar often obscures meaning.

In fact there were only two speeches. To make the copy clear and grammatical, cut 'a brace of'.

Fewer and less

'Fewer trees/less wood' is the basic distinction between number and volume. But there are traps. Some things that sound like number – because they are in the plural – don't take 'fewer': 'For next week's visit, the Queen's third to Rome, even for a meeting of less than half an hour's duration with an aged and ailing pontiff – though one who is fewer than six years older than she is – there would have been more than usually delicate diplomatic negotiations.'

Change 'fewer' to 'less' (and rewrite the sentence with fewer parentheses).

Like those of time and age, measurements of distance take 'less': 'It was less than five miles away.'

Sometimes neither 'fewer' nor 'less' will do: 'Teachers get longer holidays and work fewer hours than any other profession.'

Change 'fewer' to 'shorter': 'fewer' is logically wrong, while 'less' sounds wrong; 'shorter', on the other hand, makes a better contrast with 'longer', earlier in the sentence.

Words like 'facilities' don't take either 'fewer' or 'less': instead say 'better/worse facilities'.

That and which

The distinction between 'that' (used to define) and 'which' (the relative pronoun) is still made by some. But it would be difficult to impose the distinction on writers who don't make it. What should be imposed is consistency within sentences: what starts as a 'that' can't become a 'which' in mid-sentence.

'In part, Haider's popularity can be accounted for by the unravelling of the post-war political settlement in Europe that has destroyed the Italian Christian Democrats and which underlies some of the troubles of former Chancellor Kohl.'

Delete 'which'.

'In October he departed Radio Five Live apparently disgusted at the "Blairite consensus" that he alleged dominates the corporation and which was stifling his iconoclastic right-wing views.'

Delete 'which'.

Too many nots

Too many nots in quick succession make the reader work too hard: 'But the euro is not something Mr Brown mentions. Not so the Sun.'

Change to: 'But Mr Brown is silent about the euro. Not so the Sun.'

'"We'll find out how Will Greenwood's defence stacks up against these two fellas," said Woodward, among those who do not expect Harry Viljoen to send out his South African side with a total disregard for the game's percentages.'

Change to: '. . . Woodward, who expects Harry Viljoen to send out his South African side with an eye to the game's percentages.'

Mixed-up words

The *Spectator* columnist Taki once labelled himself an anti-Semite by accident. He used the French phrase 'soi disant', intending to describe himself as 'a so-called anti-Semite' – in fact it means 'self-styled'. A good sub would have spotted and removed the mistake.

Foreign words and phrases are often misused; so are long Latinate ones. Words like 'dilemma', 'celibate' and 'decimate' mean different things to different people. The sub's job is to ensure that readers get the writer's message. To do this you need to know how readers will interpret the word in question. Do they think that 'disinterested' means 'bored' or 'impartial'? That 'verbal' means 'to do with words' or 'spoken'?

If in doubt, play safe: change the problem word to a clearer one.

'The few sentences were effortlessly turned to evince a ripple of laughter.'

Change 'evince' to 'evoke'.

'We do not refute that some people can find them helpful.'

Change 'refute' to 'deny'.

Wrong word altogether

Always read copy several times for sense. The nonsense that follows is caused by a key word coming out wrong: 'England's backs coach Brian Ashton reckoned before the game that the team was simply failing to create the chances it was making.'

Change 'create' to 'convert'.

Ambiguity

In journalism, above all news, the greatest virtue is clarity. What exactly does the following sentence mean? Does 'since' mean 'because' or 'after'? 'Figures released by the Universities Council for the Education of Teachers show that the failure rate at one institution soared from 3 per cent to around 23 per cent since trainees this year have had to take the test on a computer rather than with a pen and paper.'

Stick to the facts: change 'since' to 'after', deleting 'have' (also delete 'around' before '23 per cent').

One and you

Mixing 'one' and 'you' in the same sentence is common in conversation – but a mistake in print: 'And surely one has to be a pretty tough cookie to have practised as a lawyer, while raising a family, while writing a book slamming your sisters.'

Change 'one has' to 'you have'.

Position of only

Putting 'only' in the wrong place can cause confusion: 'Damilola had only moved from Nigeria to London last autumn because his sister needed treatment at a London hospital.'

Does the writer want to emphasise that Damilola came to London recently or that he came because his sister was ill? In a news story (which this is) why emphasise either point? Why not let the facts speak for themselves? Delete 'only': nothing is lost.

Who and whom

'Who did you invite?' – though technically incorrect – is now considered acceptable in mainstream journalism. But doing the opposite (using 'whom' for 'who' or 'us' for 'we') is not. In the following example change 'whom' to 'who': 'It is easy to warm to the man whom the polls suggest would be the people's choice.'

Punctuation

See *English for Journalists*, Chapters 5–6 (Punctuation and Reporting speech). Here's a list of 10 common punctuation mistakes:

1   Leaving out an essential apostrophe: 'Its no use complaining.' Correct as follows: 'It's no use complaining' ('it's' is short for 'it is').

2   Putting in an unnecessary apostrophe: 'Mind your P's and Q's'/ 'Apostrophe's are difficult to use.' Correct by deleting the apostrophes (but note that 'p's and q's' would take apostrophes).

3   Putting an apostrophe in the wrong place: 'He was the peoples' champion.' Correct as follows: 'He was the people's champion.'

4   Leaving out an essential hyphen: 'He was a black cab driver.' Correct as follows: 'He was a black-cab driver' (or 'He drove a black cab').

5   Putting in an unnecessary hyphen: 'It was a commonly-observed phenomenon.' Correct by deleting the hyphen (-ly adverbs never need hyphens).

6   Putting a hyphen in the wrong place: 'They were hot dog-munching sports fans.' Correct by making 'hotdog' one word – then the hyphen is in the right place.

7   Putting more than two dashes in a sentence: 'He went up to London – by train naturally – how else? – and saw the queen.' Correct by making the first dash a comma.

8   Leaving out the query (question mark) that follows a rhetorical question: 'Have you ever thought of moving to the country.' Correct by putting in the query.

9   Leaving out the second comma in a descriptive phrase: 'He comes from Brisbane, Australia (-) and plays cricket.' Correct by putting in the comma.

10 Putting quotes marks (scare-quotes) round slang to distance the writer from it: 'Their builder was a "cowboy".' Correct by deleting the quotes – or by changing 'cowboy' to something else.

Spelling

See *English for Journalists*, Chapter 4 (Spelling).

English spelling is not easy – witness the mistakes made daily with 'ecstacy' for 'ecstasy', 'mantlepiece' for 'mantelpiece', 'harrass' for 'harass', 'concensus' for 'consensus', 'miniscule' for 'minuscule', 'supercede' for 'supersede' etc.

In theory spell-checkers, properly used, should reduce straightforward spelling mistakes to a minimum – but they can never do anything about often hilarious homophones: different words that are confused because they sound the same. Many of the examples below are taken from the *Guardian's* Corrections and clarifications column. But the first comes from a book about subediting.

'Teenage runaway Kirsty McFadden has revealed how she earned an astonishing £600 a week begging on the streets of Bristol to feed her heroine habit.' That should be 'heroin'.

'Among the more outrageous demands of employers was a request for details of one secretary's menstrual cycle so that her boss could give her a wide birth.' That should be 'berth'.

'It was rather like watching a Victorian gentleman trying to back-peddle on a penny farthing.' That should be 'pedal'.

'France is full of British ex-patriots.' That should be 'expatriates'.

'East London pubs are full of Cockney geysers.' That should be 'geezers'.

'The club are building up a head of steam, beginning to resemble the geezers of their Icelandic owners' homeland.' That should be 'geysers'.

'Right on queue the others arrived for lunch.' That should be 'cue'.

'It was suggested that Enoch Powell insighted violence.' That should be 'incited'.

'In New Labour Tony Blair holds the reigns firmly.' That should be 'reins'.

'Academics pour over statistics.' That should be 'pore'.

'Children enjoy read-allowed books.' That should be 'aloud'.

'Marianne was bearing one breast.' That should be 'baring'.

'He was the principle producer.' That should be 'principal'.

'Mr Blair sort to assuage Unionist objections.' That should be 'sought'.

'Society rung its hands.' That should be 'wrung'.

'How can you censor a man for writing well?' That should be 'censure'.

'Men strip to the waste.' That should be 'waist'.

'The flat has a rather fine rubbish shoot.' That should be 'shute'.

'People with bad backs need lumber support.' That should be 'lumbar'.

'The Romans ate door mice.' That should be 'dormice'.

Wynford Hicks

5
Subbing news and features

Copy editing is the basic subbing skill. All copy must fit the space available; must be checked to ensure it is correct; and must be rewritten where necessary for sense, readability and style. To be specific:

1   Fitting: cut or add so copy fits the space available
2   Facts: ensure that copy is accurate
3   Sense: ensure that copy is clear and readable
4   Style: ensure that copy is suitable for the page or section
5   Good English: correct grammar, spelling, punctuation etc
6   House style: put copy into house style
7   Legal and ethical problems: make copy safe.

Each of the last three points has a chapter to itself (see Chapters 3, 4 and 10).

1   Fitting copy

Before computers, subs had to master a time-consuming procedure called 'casting off' – working out how much space on the printed page a piece of copy would take up. The method was to estimate the number of words or characters in the copy and use this to work out the length on the page. The copy could then be fitted.

Alternatively – and more expensively – unfitted copy would be sent to the printers to be typeset; it would come back in long strips ('galley proofs') so that the page layout could be done and then any necessary cuts (or adds) made. As a compromise solution, some magazines had their own typist whose job was to retype submitted copy to a particular width so the subs could cast off more quickly and accurately.

Now, if there is a page layout on screen, the sub can see at a glance whether the copy fits into the allocated space – and what has to be done. Even without a page layout, a simple formula, easily learnt, converts words into space on the printed page.

Cutting

1   Try to improve the copy at the same time as you cut, so always be on the lookout for repetition, verbiage, excessive detail etc.

2   If the copy is much too long, cut large chunks before you start fiddling with detail.

3   If a news story has been properly constructed you can cut it from the end – but check first that this is so.

4   Always check that a cut doesn't destroy the logic and coherence of a piece (by removing the first stage of an argument or the first reference to something).

5   Look for titles and expressions that can be abbreviated without creating confusion.

6   Widows (one word or part of a word on a line) and other short lines at the ends of pars often make the easiest cuts.

7   Sometimes pars can be run on – but don't make them too long.

8   Remember that material cut from copy can come in handy in writing picture captions.

Adding

Cutting copy is a basic subbing skill; adding is harder, particularly if the piece is already the right length or would read even better if cut. The straightforward possibilities are:

1   First check that nothing has been cut (for space reasons) at an earlier stage.

2   Make an extra new par if this will gain a line.

3   Look for a long line at the end of a par and add a word or two to turn the line.

4   Turn common abbreviations – the US, MPs – into their long forms.

5   Use your ingenuity to replace short words and expressions by long ones – without making the piece seem padded.

2   Making copy accurate

Flair is important in subbing – but accuracy is the sine qua non. So if getting things right doesn't appeal to you, forget subbing and start thinking about doing something else.

Mistakes are particularly common in certain key areas – names, titles etc, figures and specialised vocabulary. Learn how to use reference books (see Further reading) and the internet for research (see Chapter 2, p. 13). But remember that reference books are not infallible (they can contradict each other) and out-of-date ones are often positively misleading.

The good sub is not somebody who knows more than everyone else – but is unsure exactly what they know and what they don't. That kind of person is dangerous on a subs' desk. The good sub is someone that may not know every-thing – but does know when and where to check.

The first and most obvious check is with the person who wrote the piece you're subbing. Is the name correct? Has there been a typing error? Is the dis-crepancy apparent or real? Next, as well as reference books, don't forget experi-enced colleagues, particularly fellow subs. Then, as with the all-important legal check, it may be worth consulting an outside expert.

- ALWAYS make that extra check
- NEVER introduce a new error into copy

Names, titles etc

People's names cause more trouble than anything. It's the writer's job to get names right in the first place, but the good sub checks them wherever possible. Be particularly careful with last names starting with Mac/Mc etc; with double-barrelled names (hyphen or not?); with foreign names (Daniel arap Moi) or names anglicised from other languages (Walter de la Mare/Earl De La Warr).

Remember that first names are capable of being spelt in various ways (according to national origin, family tradition or parental whim) – Ann/Anne, Anthony/Antony, Caroline/Carolyn, Catherine/Katharine, Geoffrey/Jeffrey, Gillian/Jillian, Laurence/Lawrence, Philip/Phillip, John without an h, Harriet with an extra t, Jeane just like that (as opposed to the more familiar Jean and Jeanne), Lucian (often misspelt), Aiden (as opposed to Aidan), Darian (as opposed to Darien) . . .

Titles come next, including lords and ladies, the clergy, the military and every-body else not content to be plain Mr or Mrs: unless you're 100 per cent certain of the correct form of address, check – in *Who's Who/Burke's Peerage*, *Crock-ford's Clerical Directory*, the *Army List* ... Even with Mrs there's a problem since some women prefer Ms – and some publications insist on it as a matter of house style.

Place names can trip anybody. How to remember that when Tonbridge in Kent gave its name to a nearby spa town, this became Tunbridge Wells? That Middlesbrough alone of British towns refuses to be like Loughborough (English) or Edinburgh (Scottish)? Whether there are hyphens in Newcastle under Lyme (no) and apostrophes in Bishop's Stortford and King's Langley (yes)? The common place names that cause problems are in *ODWE* but every office needs a proper gazetteer – don't rely on the AA *members' handbook*.

Among other curiosities to confuse the unwary are the colleges of Oxford and Cambridge: Magdalen college, Oxford, contrasts with Magdalene college, Cambridge; and Christ Church (no college), Oxford, with Christ's college, Cambridge. At Cambridge Peterhouse also does not have college in its title while Emmanuel college contrasts with Emanuel school in south London. Again *ODWE* has the solution to many (though not all) of these problems.

Literary quotations should be checked in a dictionary of quotations since jour-nalists (like most people) often get them wrong. Money may be the root of all evil but, as Leslie Sellers noted, the Bible said something subtler: 'The love of money is the root of all evil.'

Be careful of records – the first, the longest etc – being claimed in copy. Check them in the *Guinness Book of Records*; then if the book agrees, quote it in support of the claim.

Figures

Although subs don't cast off nowadays, they still need basic numeracy. Otherwise they're likely to miss the numerical and mathematical mistakes that crop up in copy.

The simplest mistakes involve losing a nought, say, in a sum of money, or putting the decimal point in the wrong place, or mistyping one digit in a phone number. As so often in subbing, the way to reduce error in figures is to read carefully in the first place and check as much as possible. On some magazines subs check phone numbers before publication – by phoning the number.

Percentages are often a problem. Say the number of people using mobile phones goes up from 60 per cent of the population in 2002 to 75 per cent in 2003. That may look like an increase of 15 per cent but it isn't: in fact it is an increase of a quarter of the original number (60 per cent of the population plus 15 per cent of it) – that is, an increase of 25 per cent.

Some reporters seem to believe that the point of figures is to impress – the bigger the better. A band of 10 bank robbers get 10-year sentences, but they must be totted up so the reporter can proclaim: 'The defendants were jailed for a total of 100 years.' What can that possibly mean – except that there were 10 of them? (It also devalues consecutive sentences that people charged with multiple crimes can receive.)

In reporting surveys some journalists insist on jumbling together percentages, fractions and decimals – to brighten up their copy, no doubt. But the effect is confusion for the reader. It's easier and makes more sense to compare like with like.

In general, percentages are harder to cope with than fractions and fractions are harder to cope with than whole numbers. So whenever possible say 'one person in 10' rather than 'one tenth' or '10 per cent'.

Be careful with averages. An average tends to be somewhere in the middle of a set of figures. So it's hardly news to write: 'Almost 50 per cent of British people have shorter than average holidays.' The same point applies to the IQ scale, whose midpoint is 100. About half the population will have an IQ score lower than 100.

Don't preface precise figures with approximations. You can't logically have 'about 116 people' or 'around 23.3 per cent'. Resist the temptation to exaggerate when approximating: if your intro says 'nearly 100 people' while the story refers to 85, it just looks ridiculous.

Then there are phrases like 'a substantial number', 'a significant minority', 'a large proportion' and 'a high percentage of the population'. Avoid them: they pretend to be impressive and precise but they are empty words. If you're using figures, be precise.

In dates 'between' should be followed by 'and'; 'from' by 'to'. It's a common mistake to write 'between 1979–97' or 'from 1979–97'. That should be 'between 1979 and 1997' or 'from 1979 to 1997' or 'in 1979–97'.

Specialist vocabulary

If you sub on a specialist title or section you will have to learn its specialist vocabulary quickly or you won't be able to function at all. But readers of general publications and sections are also entitled to accuracy. Two contributors to the *Journalist's* Chief sub column have complained about widespread ignorance of their specialisms. First Mike Woof on the construction industry:

> You've seen the intro: 'The bulldozers went in at dawn to demolish the building.'
>
> In fact, they probably didn't because bulldozers are rarely used in demolition work. This is a common mistake but one that's easily avoided. If you want to describe the machine, call it demolition equipment or heavy plant, though for what it is worth, this industry now mainly uses excavators fitted with demolition attachments.
>
> Calling a piece of excavation machinery a mechanical digger is usually incorrect (most are hydraulic); this mistake occurs because journalists confuse the words 'mechanical' and 'mechanised'. If a machine is used to dig a hole, call it a digger or an excavator.
>
> The term 'dumper truck' is used but it is always wrong. There are dumpers – small machines used mainly by house-builders with the skip (the bit that carries the dirt) in front of the driver and a load capacity of up to 7 tonnes. And there are dump trucks – big things, with capacities of up to 300 tonnes, used in civil engineering, quarrying or open-pit mining.

Now Bernard Eccles on horoscope columns:

> To start with, the person who interprets a horoscope is an astrologer, not an astrologist. There is no such thing as an astrologist, though the word appears in print with depressing regularity. Astrologers are very proud of studying the only -ology which has -ers instead of -ists.
>
> Don't confuse astronomers, who scan galaxies for signs of alien life, with astrologers who look at charts to predict the future. Astrologers labelled astronomers shrug it off with a smile, but astronomers labelled astrologers go ballistic.
>
> The signs of the zodiac seldom give subs trouble, but the associated adjectives do. There seems to be a strange compulsion to change Arian to Arien, no matter how often the poor astrologer writes the former – and I have known one features editor who would personally change it to Aryan. (Mind you, this person used to change Saturn to Satan as well, so perhaps there was a deeper problem somewhere.) The correct version is Arian (follower of Arius), despite the e in Aries, as *ODWE* confirms.

3   Rewriting for sense: news

It's obvious that all copy has to make sense to the reader and be readable, whether it's written by an amateur, a trainee, a star columnist or an experienced professional, and whether it's published in a broadsheet or a tabloid newspaper, a trade weekly or a glossy consumer monthly, a company newsletter or on the internet.

But this point is not as simple to apply as it sounds. Some readers of a publication know more and are more literate than others. And some writers are inclined to justify obscurity on the grounds that 'their' readers will get the message. According to legend, a past economics editor of the *Times* once defended a dense and difficult piece to a critical subeditor on the grounds that it had been written with three particular people in mind – 'and you're not one of them'. (Today's *Times* has a much more popular approach.)

With experience subs develop a feel for readers of their publication, knowing when to explain or simplify – at the risk of irritating the knowledgeable – and when to let writers have their head. In general, there is more scope for individual tricks of style in features, particularly personal columns. By contrast in news writing and instructional copy – how to make an omelette or change a plug – the argument for clarity is overwhelming.

Let the story tell itself without unnecessary repetition, circumlocution, ambiguity – in other words clutter. In general choose short, simple words in short, simple sentences and paragraphs. Prefer the active to the passive, the direct to the indirect, the concrete to the abstract. Avoid pomposity and formal language – sub news stories into plain English.

In news the intro is all-important. Get it right and you tell the story in a simple form and make the reader want to stay with you; get it wrong and you either confuse them or lose them immediately. Three of the biggest faults in news intros are: missing the point, trying to say too much and overstating the case.

Missing the point

Read the following piece submitted as a news story to *Police Review* magazine and ask yourself whether the intro does what an intro should do – convey the essence of the story.

> The Government will shortly announce its decision on the possible repeal of the power in the Magistrates' Courts Act under which detention in police cells may be ordered for up to four days for drink-drive defendants.

> From the tone of exchanges in the House of Commons last week, however, it looks as if the Government has already decided to abolish

this particular power of the courts. Home Office Minister David Mellor indicated that he did not believe policemen should be used as jailers 'when we have a prison system to carry out that function'.

He was responding to a call from the MP for Leicester East, Peter Bruinvels, for people to be deterred from drinking and driving. The MP claimed that more than 1,000 people lose their lives each year through drink-driving related offences. He wanted immediate prison sentences to be imposed.

David Mellor said that there was no intention of going soft on drinking and driving, but that the issue was whether it should be appropriate for the courts to sentence people to remain in police cells rather than to imprisonment.

This intro fails because it certainly does not convey the essence of the story. Indeed it tells the reader nothing interesting or relevant – it just says that soon there will be some news. So if you're subbing the story, there is no point tinkering with the existing intro: you need to start all over again.

Buried in the story are two points on which to base an intro: one, David Mellor has criticised the practice of detaining drink-drive offenders in police stations; two, his statement suggests that the government is about to end the practice.

While the second point may be more interesting, it's always difficult to make a supposition or a guess the basis of an intro: whereas a confident prediction ('this will happen') works well, a hedged bet ('it may happen') doesn't. So keep it simple and lead on the first point:

The police should not be used as jailers when there is a prison system to carry out that function, Home Office minister David Mellor told the House of Commons.

He was responding to a call from Leicester East MP Peter Bruinvels for people to be deterred from drinking and driving by immediate sentences.

Mellor's words suggest that the government have decided to abolish the power of magistrates to detain drink-drive offenders in police cells for up to four days. A decision on this is expected soon.

A couple of details to note here – apart from the general tightening of the copy. The first part of the rewritten intro has no quote marks. There is no need for them because the sentence is not a quote: as a concise version of what the speaker said, it doesn't necessarily use their actual words.

Also, 'defendants' in the original has become 'offenders' in the subbed version: this is because defendants cannot be sentenced until they become 'offenders' – that is, are found guilty.

Trying to say too much

Does the following news intro tell the story in a nutshell? Or has the writer been unable to resist the temptation of trying to explain the background to the story at the same time as telling it?

> Secondary school pupils do not want to be taught about politics and the workings of parliament, which were a key element of the plans by the education secretary, David Blunkett, for compulsory citizenship lessons, announced two weeks ago. Rather, the pupils want more advice on dealing with personal relationships.
>
> In a clear signal that they would like more practical help to cope with impending adulthood, youngsters are also demanding more information about managing money, such as opening bank accounts, according to a MORI survey, to be published shortly.

There is a lot of clutter here. For example, why bother to specify that Blunkett's plans were announced 'two weeks ago' and that the MORI survey will be published 'shortly'? In the first case the reader does not need to be told or reminded exactly when the plans were announced. In the second 'shortly' says nothing at all.

The biggest obstacle to a straightforward reading of the intro is the parenthesis describing the background, 'which were a key element of the plans by the education secretary, David Blunkett, for compulsory citizenship lessons'. Then in the par that follows there's a further long-winded context-creating phrase, 'in a clear signal that they would like more practical help to cope with impending adulthood'.

There's a much simpler and punchier way of approaching the story:

> Young people think they should be taught more about personal relationships and managing money but are not particularly keen on politics, according to a MORI survey.
>
> These findings will not please education secretary David Blunkett who has announced plans to introduce compulsory citizenship lessons in secondary schools.

Overstating the case

Here's an intro that sounds lively, although it's a bit long. The positive effect comes from the accumulated colourful detail in the list and the cleverly recycled cliché 'shoot-from-the-lip'. Some people may object to the extended martial metaphor ('defeated . . . shoot-from-the-lip . . . vanquished . . . army'), but it fits Giuliani's aggressive approach.

> Rudolph Giuliani, the mayor who has defeated New York's strip clubs, sex shops, hotdog stalls, squeegee merchants and jaywalkers with his popular shoot-from-the-lip style, was finally vanquished himself yesterday by an army of urban gardeners led by an actress who came to prominence singing in gay bath houses.

The intro would be tighter without 'himself' and the clumsy bit after 'actress'. But that is not what sinks it. To see what does, you have to read the piece. Somewhere in the middle is the following par:

> Some strip clubs and sex shops have been forced to close but many others have found ways of complying with the law and staying open. Hotdog stalls continue to flourish and jaywalking goes unpunished. But New York's top tourist attraction – Times Square – has been purged of sleaze.

Reality turns out to be more complicated than the intro suggests: the mayor has not in fact 'defeated New York's strip clubs, sex shops, hotdog stalls, squeegee merchants and jaywalkers'. In simple words, as it stands, the intro is nonsense. So what is to be done? If you're subbing the piece do you start all over again with a fresh intro? Or do you cut from the intro all the examples that are contradicted in the text?

It would be a pity to lose the idea of the intro – it's a good one. But once you start cutting the weak examples you'll find there won't be much left. The solution is to replace the key word 'defeated' by something like 'attacked':

> Rudolph Giuliani, the mayor who has attacked New York's strip clubs, sex shops, hotdog stalls, squeegee merchants and jaywalkers in his popular shoot-from-the-lip style, was vanquished yesterday – by an army of urban gardeners and an actress.

This example illustrates a principle of subbing: if the simplest solution involving the minimum of work and the minimum of interference does the trick, always choose it. Never undertake a massive rewrite for the sake of rewriting.

Unfortunately, the subbing work on this piece is not over yet because there is an important fault in the second quoted par: it's got two 'buts' in it, often a sign of faulty structure. The par goes: (A) strip clubs and sex shops close BUT (B) some stay open AND (B) hotdog stalls and jaywalking carry on BUT (A) Times Square has been purged.

As the writing doubles back on itself the reader is expected to follow its tortured logic. The sub's job is to save the reader the trouble by a simple change of order:

> New York's top tourist attraction – Times Square – has been purged of sleaze, and some strip clubs and sex shops elsewhere have been forced

to close. But many others have found ways of complying with the law and staying open. Hotdog stalls continue to flourish and jaywalking goes unpunished.

4   Rewriting for style: features

Much journalism is, at least partly, entertainment. If it's well written – so that people who buy a particular publication find it readable – then it can do its other job, which may be to inform, to argue a case, to educate . . .

Professional feature writers, particularly columnists, are usually paid well because they write well (and celebrities who can't write have ghost writers to do the hard work for them). But even good feature writers sometimes need help with the odd phrase.

Amateurs, on the other hand, may be commissioned – or have their unsolicited pieces accepted – because of their knowledge of the subject rather than their writing ability. And this can mean a lot of work for the sub if what is expected is a high standard of writing.

Below is a typical example of the kind of thing a sub on a specialist magazine often has to cope with: one continuous paragraph of long-winded, turgid prose, full of passives and pompous expressions – the opposite of lively, readable journalism. An advantage you have as a sub is that almost always you're expected to make substantial cuts at the rewriting stage – so you can afford to junk large sections of what you start off with.

Read the piece that follows, deciding which bits are essential and which you can do without – and of course try to find an idea for the intro.

> Following a complete refurbishment of the Solihull Police Social Club, funds began accumulating and it was decided that it would be a good idea to purchase a holiday venue for the use of club members. Sergeant Alan Griffin put forward the idea of a villa in Spain which would allow an all the year round letting period. Enquiries with our Bank encouraged us they were prepared to back us financially, and thought it a good idea. Over the next few months myself and Alan Griffin went on several trips to the Costa Del Sol and looked at hundreds of properties. On return we put a choice of several villas in various locations on the Costa Del Sol before the Committee, with literature, photographs etc, and it was decided to purchase at San Juan, Capistrano, Nerja. Consideration had been given for the need to have somewhere that could be managed on our behalf and with that in mind we actually purchased just a plot of land for the villa to be built. San Juan, Capistrano, is about one hour's drive from Malaga Airport, in a quaint little fishing village called Nerja.

Capistrano itself is a purpose-built village with excellent facilities and beautifully laid out gardens. The villa itself comprises of two bedrooms and a large lounge/kitchen area, the complete roof is a sunroof with access by a spiral staircase and there is a large veranda. We also have our own private garden to which entrance is gained by a lockable gate. The villa will sleep up to seven persons. Opposite the villa and less than 50 yards away is an excellent new complex comprising of squash courts, swimming pool, restaurant yet to be completed, and the administration buildings, supermarket, a bar which is underground and has views into the swimming pool. Total cost of the villa was some £30,000 and at the time of writing is paid for. We have experienced no letting problems since the villa was opened for use. Our charges range from £300 peak period to £150 during the winter months. We have also made an excellent contact for car hire at Malaga, with special rates for police officers.

Where do you start? With the intro, of course: try to find a way of getting to the point quickly – without necessarily throwing away the idea contained in the original. But in style the piece needs a complete makeover: change everything except the facts and figures. This is what was published:

When the Solihull Police Social Club found themselves with money in the bank, they decided to invest in their own Spanish holiday villa. Two of them went to the Costa del Sol and looked at hundreds of properties; the club finally chose a site near the charming fishing village of Nerja – about an hour's drive from Malaga airport.

The purpose-built villa sleeps seven and includes a large living-room, sunroof, veranda and private garden. Less than 50 yards away there's a swimming pool with squash courts, bar etc.

Rates vary from £150 a week in the winter to £300 in high summer and there's a good car-hire firm in Malaga with special rates for police officers. The villa cost £30,000 and was bought with the help of a bank loan; this has now been paid off.

Further details from:

Changing from the first person to the third is a great help here and so is the obvious step of introducing paragraphs. Otherwise the rewrite is in everyday English rather than a mixture of policespeak and estate agent's blurb. Finally, never forget that vital last par – the one that tells the reader what to do next if they want more information. This is just as important as coming up with a lively intro.

Once you've got used to doing them, rewrites like the one above present fewer problems than features which are broadly on the right lines but need some adjustment. The hardest thing for a sub to acquire is judgment: when to rewrite and when to leave alone.

What's wrong – and right – with the following short feature written for the junior section of a Sunday newspaper magazine?

> Scrap metal yards are hardly the obvious places to practise nature conservation, but in Yapton, a small village in Sussex, there is a rather unusual exception. The Yapton Metal Company owned by my parents deals in non-ferrous metals and all kinds of second-hand goods. I run the business and am also a keen naturalist. I try to observe everything that grows, crawls, creeps or flies in the yard.
>
> Here, butterflies haunt the buddleia and thistles that grow out of the gaps among piles of zinc and stainless steel, and up to 14 species have been recorded in a year. Rabbits have happily colonised the vast bramble complex behind sheds made out of doors and gas cookers, and over 50 species of birds are seen each year.
>
> Every year swallows nest in one or more of the sheds. Wrens or robins rear their young successfully in a multitude of strange places – old kettles, lavatory cisterns, even the old chimney of a boiler. Last year, a lesser-spotted woodpecker caused much interest by drumming on the pole holding up the telephone wires across the yard, and in the spring a female blackbird reared a family of four in an ingenious nest built on a bicycle wheel.
>
> I am currently working on a complete natural history of the scrap yard and, when complete, the quantity and variety of flora and fauna should be impressive if not unique. The history will indicate what is surviving in one of the most unlikely ecological habitats.

The intro is based on the obvious idea – the surprising juxtaposition of scrap metal and wildlife – but the end of the sentence, 'there is a rather unusual exception', is weak. Then unnecessary and misleading detail is given about the Yapton Metal Company, which is said to deal in 'non-ferrous metals' – this suggests that it *doesn't* deal in ferrous metals so how to explain the reference to 'stainless steel' in the next par? And '*all kinds* of second-hand goods'? Surely not.

The main part of the feature – observed detail of scrapyard wildlife – is its strength. There are some flaws to remove – eg the thistles are said to grow 'out of the gaps among' piles of zinc; the swallows are said to nest in 'one or more' of the sheds; an old boiler chimney is described as 'the old chimney of a boiler'; the conjunction 'and' is misused twice in the second par; and why is the nesting blackbird separated from the swallows, wrens and robins? But the flaws, once spotted, are easily removed: this is routine subbing.

At first glance the biggest problem in the piece is the final par. It has very little content and is full of mistakes – eg repetition ('complete . . . complete'), bad grammar ('when complete, the quantity . . .'), pretentious and formal language ('flora and fauna . . . impressive if not unique . . . indicate'). But in a rewrite all this clutter disappears:

> You wouldn't expect to be able to study nature in a scrapyard – but at Yapton, a village in Sussex, I do. I run the Yapton Metal Company, which is owned by my parents, and I am also a keen naturalist. I try to observe everything that grows, crawls, creeps or flies in the yard and I'm working on a natural history of it.
>
> Here butterflies haunt the buddleia and thistles which grow among piles of zinc and stainless steel; up to 14 species have been recorded in a year. Rabbits have colonised the vast bramble complex that lies behind sheds made from doors and gas cookers. Then there are the birds.
>
> More than 50 species visit the yard. Swallows nest in the sheds. Wrens and robins adopt all sorts of strange nesting places: kettles, lavatory cisterns – even an old boiler chimney. Last year a blackbird reared a family of four in an ingenious nest built on a bicycle wheel. And we heard a lesser spotted woodpecker drumming on the telephone pole.

There's a curiosity in the final sentence. Some reference books give 'lesser spotted' a hyphen – but this could be misleading: the bird is in fact the smaller of two spotted woodpeckers (it doesn't have fewer spots) so the hyphen is best left out.

Now, before reading Chapter 7 (on headline writing), write a headline for the feature above in between two and four words. Then compare yours with the ones discussed on p. 77.

Wynford Hicks

6
Editing quotes and letters

On 4 September 2000 the *Guardian* ran a front-page interview with Chris Woodhead, then the chief inspector of schools in England, with this quote prominently displayed: 'We can't have a situation where young people are kept for longer and longer at school, and at greater public expense, but who end up knowing no more than those in the past did who left school younger.'

In next day's paper there was a sneering letter in response: 'As someone who is of the same generation as Mr Woodhead, I question how a person whose usage of language and grammar are so poor can presume to criticise others. The quote given on your front page did little to enhance his standing in my eyes. Does anyone know if Mr Woodhead gained a pass in English literature and/or grammar at O and A level?'

So Woodhead is made to look ridiculous. But what about the *Guardian* subs? Having – for whatever reason – highlighted rather than corrected Woodhead's bad grammar they fail to correct the illiteracy of his critic who follows a singular noun (usage) by a plural verb (are).

There are people who say that on principle quotes and letters should not be edited at all – but this tiny minority does not include the *Guardian*. For example, the Woodhead quote was changed when it was highlighted as a pull quote. In the text it read: 'We *cannot* have a situation where young people are kept for longer and longer at school, and at greater *and greater* public expense, but who end up *in fact* knowing no more than *people* in the past did who left school younger.'

The *Guardian*'s own stylebook (available on its website) says: 'People we write about are allowed to speak in their own, not necessarily the *Guardian*'s, style, but be sensitive: do not, for example, expose someone to ridicule for dialect or grammatical errors.' And the letters page includes the warning: 'We may edit letters.'

Quotes

It goes without saying that direct quotes should be authentic – recognisable as the person's own words. So it would be pointless and silly to make them conform rigidly to house-style rules on such things as contractions, slang and obscenity.

But that does not mean quotes are not subbed. For example, it is standard practice for subs to condense quotes when they are used as pull quotes so that they fit the space, read better and have more impact. Subs should also ensure that quotes, in whatever form, make sense, are coherent and don't embarrass the speaker.

In speech many people ramble and make false starts; think *as* rather than *before* they speak; say things they wouldn't write; make silly mistakes. Take 'one' and 'you': in speech people often mix them up saying: 'One does this on Monday and you do that on Tuesday.' In print this should be: 'You do this on Monday and you do that on Tuesday.'

Style books often acknowledge the point. The *Yorkshire Evening Post* says: 'Problems arise in quotes that are ungrammatical because English is not the speaker's best subject or statements are badly contorted because the speaker has had little time to prepare. A little "tidying up" while preserving accuracy is the best treatment.'

And the *Times* says the same thing, although its emphasis is different: 'Direct quotes should be corrected only to remove the solecisms and other errors that occur in speech but look silly in print.'

The *YEP* goes on to make an exception of court reporting. It says: 'Quotes with a legal significance are best left alone – no tidying up. Timothy Evans (hanged for a murder he did not commit) said "Christie done it." These are the words the jury weighed and rejected. The intellectual difference between the two men figured strongly at the inquiry 16 years after Evans was hanged.'

Another problem is words that mean different things to different people (see pp. 27–8). If words with more than one meaning are used in a quote, the sub should first decide whether the context makes the meaning clear. For example, take the word 'celibate' (unmarried or abstaining from sex). If the person quoted is discussing the question of sex inside marriage, the word 'celibate' will obviously mean abstaining from sex. But if the issue is the Catholic Church's rules governing their priests, there is room for confusion: Catholic priests may not marry – and are not supposed to have sex either.

If there is confusion the sub should remove it. There are three possibilities: first, cut (the quote may make perfectly good sense without the confusing word); second, substitute a clear word for the confusing one; third, rewrite the quote in indirect speech. Editorial policy may determine which move you make here: in some offices, eg broadsheet newspapers, the third move may be preferred to the second; whereas a popular paper or magazine may insist on the second. It is not the sub's function to make editorial policy but to carry it out: if in doubt, always check with your chief sub or editor.

In the reporting of politicians' speeches a case can be made for quoting verbatim rather than tidying up when the effect is comic, as so often with George W. Bush (see box on p. 63). But *Hansard* reporters routinely finish MPs' sentences for them and tidy up their grammar. In general, where the reporter does not do this, the sub should.

Some cases are marginal. If the England football manager tells a post-match press conference that conditions were 'slippy', some papers will use the exact word while others change it to 'slippery'. This is a marginal case because in both versions the meaning is clear and in neither is the speaker made to look silly: essentially, the judgment is one of style.

But with interviews the issue is clear cut. People have the right to be treated fairly, so quotes should not be invented – and equally they should not have the effect (whether intentionally or not) of embarrassing the speaker.

Here in a story about tests for trainee teachers is a quote from somebody who could be embarrassed:

> Trainee teacher Stephen Partington, who has a first class honours degree in English, took his test yesterday and passed. Speaking before the test he said: 'The whole thing is very patronising and insulting. I'm a strong believer in state education but if I were to fail this test I won't be able to set foot in a classroom.'

In the final sentence 'were' should be followed by 'wouldn't' (or 'won't' should have the simpler 'if I fail' before it). Whether the speaker or the reporter made the mistake (by misquoting the speaker) is irrelevant: the sub should tidy up the grammar.

Here's another example where the person interviewed is made to look silly by the incompetence of feature writer and/or sub. The interviewee is toastmaster Ivor Spencer, trainer of butlers and now of personal assistants. He is quoted as saying: 'There honestly is not a lot of difference between being a butler or being a PA. There is a lot of crossover in the way you deal with the person for whom you are working.'

The tucked-in preposition used with 'whom' shows that Spencer wants to be 'correct' – an extra reason why the 'or' that follows 'between' should be changed to 'and'.

Unedited quotes from George W. Bush

I've coined new words, like misunderstanding and Hispanically.
(29 March 2001)

You teach a child to read and he or her will be able to pass a literacy test.
(21 February 2001)

There's no such thing as legacies. At least, there is a legacy, but I'll never see it. (31 January 2001)

I am mindful not only of preserving executive powers for myself, but for predecessors as well. (29 January 2001)

My pro-life position is I believe there's life. (23 January 2001)

I do remain confident in Linda. She'll make a fine labor secretary. From what I've read in the press accounts, she's perfectly qualified. (8 January 2001)

Families is where our nation finds hope, where wings take dream.
(18 October 2000)

I know the human being and fish can coexist peacefully. (29 September 2000)

I will have a foreign-handed foreign policy. (27 September 2000)

They have miscalculated me as a leader. (13 September 2000)

Well, I think if you say you're going to do something and don't do it, that's trustworthiness. (30 August 2000)

We cannot let terrorists and rogue nations hold this nation hostile or hold our allies hostile. (30 August 2000)

States should have the right to enact reasonable laws and restrictions particularly to end the inhumane practice of ending a life that otherwise could live. (29 June 2000)

The fact that he relies on facts – says things that are not factual – are going to undermine his campaign. (4 March 2000)

Sources: *Times* (23 April 2001); *Guardian* (4 November 2000), extracted from Slate **http://politics.slate.msn.com/Features/ bushisms/bushisms.asp** by Jacob Weisberg

Later in the interview a tucked-in preposition trips Spencer into another mistake. He says of PAs: 'They need to develop a manner which is courteous and in keeping with whom they are dealing.'

Now read it again: yes, it needs another 'with'. Don't blame Spencer – being pompous isn't a crime; he has no need to apologise if English is not his best subject. Instead blame the sub who has failed to tidy up Spencer's grammar: English should be his or hers.

Like copy in general, quotes are often too long and/or confused because they try to cover too much ground. The writer reduces the impact of the quote by starting it too early or finishing it too late or running several points together.

Here's a quote from an interview with Becky Cancea, now administrator for the England women's rugby team, on her previous job at Thames Valley university:

> 'I became the sports development officer, running all the university's sports and encouraging students to get involved. However, it has become much harder because students now have to work part-time to pay their fees, and so have no time for sports. And these days, students are focusing much more on getting good degrees. But we did a lot of good work and after four years I wanted to broaden my knowledge.'

The quotable bit here is: 'Students now have to work part-time to pay their fees, and so have no time for sports. And [they] are focusing much more on getting good degrees.' The first sentence ('I became . . .') isn't worth quoting because it is routine information; the last sentence ('But we did a lot of good work . . .') confuses the issue by introducing a new point.

Also note the excessive use of 'however/but/and' here – a sign of things being run together.

Here's a subbed version of the par:

> Becky worked as Thames Valley's sports development officer, running all the university's sports and encouraging students to get involved. She's proud of what she achieved but says: 'It has become much harder because students now have to work part-time to pay their fees, and so have no time for sports. And they are focusing much more on getting good degrees.'

After four years Becky left Thames Valley to broaden her knowledge . . .

There are several small changes to note: 'However' in quote has become 'but' out of quote; 'these days' has been cut; and the second 'students' has been changed to 'they'. In this kind of routine editing of quotes there is no need to highlight the changes by using square brackets to show insertion or three dots to show deletion. Keep these devices for formal documents and statements.

Sometimes, having started quoting, the writer doesn't know what to do next – except to go on quoting. The piece turns into a succession of quoted pars. In the Ivor Spencer interview there are nine successive pars – about 450 words – in continuous direct quote.

Aware of this problem, the writer may break up a succession of quoted pars by suddenly inserting 'He added'. This phrase can of course be used to mean something – to show an afterthought, say, or with 'but' to emphasise a contrast. But by itself it is inept: it says nothing more than 'He also said' – which is the effect of the quote mark that starts each new par in continuous quote.

Clearly, an essential subbing skill is turning quotes into indirect reported speech (for technical details see the chapter on reporting speech in *English for Journalists*). Here it's worth stressing the obvious point that you can always summarise quotes in indirect speech if tidying up causes difficulty – but you must never do the reverse: indirect speech can never be used as the raw material for a concocted quote.

In subbing quotes – and readers' letters – the key word is accuracy: the exact meaning of the original must be preserved. In condensing and clarifying a quote or a letter you must never change the emphasis. So if somebody makes a statement that is qualified in some way, you remove the qualification at your peril.

A politician who says 'We have to explain the vision coherently and not simply rely on well-worn methods of campaigning . . .' is liable to complain if the word 'simply' is cut when he's quoted. Peter Mandelson did. And a reader whose original letter refers to 'one element missing from the prime minister's very welcome speech on the environment' is liable to complain if the words 'very welcome' disappear from the published version.

Letters

Readers' letters should always be checked, tidied up and put into house style. They often need cutting so that they make one point rather than several or make their one point clearly. And occasionally they need extensive rewriting.

Although some people say that letters for publication should remain the personal expression of the sender, most newspapers and magazines do in fact rewrite where necessary. The alternative would be to exclude from publication the opinions of those who don't write very well (or subject readers to unreadable material).

Consider the following example, included here exactly as it came into the *Police Review* office. As you read it, ask yourself three questions: whether on the grounds of its content, all or part of it should be published; whether it could possibly be published without being rewritten; and how you would go about doing it.

In reply to a letter printed in PR on 5th October, I was somewhat diss-apointed to say the least to read PC R Hensworth's letter regarding the Special Constabulary and feel many other Specials will have felt much as I did. Firstly, everyone has to start somewhere, even PC Hemsworth had to be shown what to do when he first joined the job, or was he born a policeman! I really must say I'm not surprised forces are having such trouble recruiting specials if there are many regulars like our friend, who simply do not give anyone a chance to prove what they may or may not be able to do, but just make disparaging remarks and derogatory comments because it makes him feel good, to dig at Specials.

Secondly don't you think that the blame should not lie with the Specials themselves, in the West Midlands a Special Constable is placed with a regular officer if possible and if not, the newer Special Constable is usually in the company of someone with at least two years experience.

What PC Hemsworth wrote in his letter was not only unkind, but also very thoughtless, specials up and down the Country turn out every week for football matches and other social events, such as Town parades, fairs, Carnivals, rememberance Parades etc, when no one seems to complain in these situations, and if he really thinks the recruitment of more specials will harm the job, why doesn't he leave. He doesn't think about all the man hours Specials put in and don't get paid for, how would he feel to be criticised under those circumstances.

I am a Special and have been so for some four years, only because I am too small to become a regular officer, but until he has been in the posi-tion of a special, and been made to feel as a Special feels in these circumstances he will never understand.

Further more his comments about very little training are groundless, training is continued throughout the life of a Special Constable, we don't get 16 weeks, end of matter, our lectures go on month and month, year after year, sure we don't get as much training as the Regular force, but if the Home Office don't like the Specials why don't they allow all Specials to become regular officers, no they wouldn't like that either they'd have to pay us all the same as PC Hemsworth.

Further more I am as I said a serving Special Constable and proud of it, I will continue to work with the West Midlands Police as long as I am allowed to, and am full of nothing but praise for policemen in this force, they are totally understanding which is something I cannot say for PC Hemsworth.

The letter was published on the grounds that it raised a number of points of interest to the *Police Review* readership – which of course includes special constables. But the subbed version was very different from the original letter:

> I was disappointed, to say the least, to read PC R Hemsworth's letter (PR October 5) about the Special Constabulary. First, everyone has to start somewhere – even PC Hemsworth had to be shown what to do when he first joined the job, or was he born a policeman?
>
> Second, the blame for a new special's inexperience should not lie with the specials themselves. In the West Midlands a special is placed with a regular officer if possible and, if not, the newer special is usually in the company of someone with at least two years' experience.
>
> What PC Hemsworth wrote was not only unkind but also very thoughtless: specials up and down the country turn out every week for football matches and other events such as town parades, fairs, carnivals, remembrance parades etc. No one seems to complain about this.
>
> Furthermore his comments about very little training are groundless. Training is continued throughout the life of a special. We don't just get 16 weeks – our lectures go on month after month, year after year.
>
> I am a serving special constable and proud of it. I will continue to work with the West Midlands Police as long as I am allowed to, and have nothing but praise for policemen in this force. They are totally understanding – which is something I cannot say for PC Hemsworth.

How do you start? First, a few routine points. Whenever a reader's letter refers to a previous one, check back with the original: you may find that letter two misquotes or misrepresents letter one – in which case it's obviously a mistake to print letter two without amendment. Unless you are effectively the letters editor, always refer points like this to your editor or department head.

In this case you would also be able to establish that of the two spellings in letter two 'Hemsworth' is the one in letter one. You would also be able to pinpoint one of Hemsworth's complaints – that new specials are too inexperienced to be any use. This is the only point the sub has added to the letter. Essentially, as with so much subbing, this is a cutting job.

Remember that if letter-writer number two libels letter-writer one it's your – and your publication's – problem. Subs must always be on the lookout for legal problems in copy including letters.

As well as rewriting, you will of course need to tidy up the grammar, spelling and punctuation, follow house style and use both common sense and specialist knowledge, whether yours or your colleagues'. This letter includes a piece of jargon – 'the job' to mean police work – which it would be crass to change. This is the kind of thing apprentice subs need to be extra careful about.

In rewriting this kind of letter concentrate on cutting to leave the bits that work. Try to keep the flavour of the original rather than introduce your own. Look for everyday, colloquial expressions such as 'I was disappointed, to say the least'. Take away any words that weaken the sentence (eg the pompous 'somewhat') and you have a strong start.

There's a strong finish, too, which is there in the original; it just needs the dash to make it work better: 'They are totally understanding – which is more than I can say for PC Hemsworth.'

Let the letter writer make their point, then stop them when they lose control and start frothing at the mouth. Three of the four substantial cuts come after a point has been made; they stop the letter degenerating into a rant.

The fourth big cut – the par in which the letter writer says he's too small to be a regular officer – seems to break a journalistic rule. Aren't shocks and surprises the stuff of journalism? If you were writing or subbing a feature on specials – who are they? what makes them tick? – or profiling the letter writer, you could hardly turn down the opportunity to explore and develop this point.

But in the context of the letter the par adds nothing and merely makes the writer look ridiculous and pathetic. So it's a good cut.

If there's any criticism to be made of editing a reader's letter in this way it's that you risk giving a falsely favourable impression of the writer. But if they are enabled to make their point effectively, and the reader gets a more coherent argument, what's the problem?

Some letters, which are published to entertain rather than to contribute to debate, are routinely rewritten by subeditors; the writers never complain because they're paid a fee and expect their drafts to be improved.

The *Reader's Digest* feature 'Life's Like That' depends on a steady flow of anecdotes contributed by readers. The fee paid for each one is £200 – far higher than rates paid to professional journalists on most other publications. Below are two examples of rewritten letters published by *Reader's Digest*:

> When one of my clerks came in to hand in her notice, she told me that she and her husband had been granted the tenancy of a small country pub. I asked her if it was old-fashioned.
>
> 'No,' she replied. 'But it will be when we have modernised it.'

> Although I knew I had put on a few pounds, I didn't consider myself overweight until the day I decided to clean my refrigerator. I sat on a chair in front of the appliance and reached in to wipe the back wall. While I was in this position, my teenage son came into the kitchen. 'Hello, Mum,' he said. 'What are you doing, having lunch?'
>
> I started my diet that day.

And now a letter in the raw state:

> My daughter Heather, aged 4, had just acquired a toy yacht and, on our first visit to the local pond, she pushed it out from the side. There was no wind and after travelling a short distance it was becalmed. I was wondering how to retrieve it when a young man, having seen our dilemma, came over and offered to try and help by using his radio-controlled paddle steamer. He was able to demonstrate his expertise by bringing the angle of the paddle housing against the yacht and managed to bring them both to the side.
>
> Heather was so delighted at having her boat retrieved that she forgot all about the person who had come to our rescue. I gave her a gentle reminder, 'Heather, aren't you going to thank the gentleman for what he did?' Her response was to say, 'Oh!' and then bending almost double, she addressed a little model sailor on the deck of the steamer, 'Thank you very much for getting my boat for me!'

How does the sub proceed here? First, the model is clear: get to the punchline as quickly and deftly as possible; unlike a news story, say, a 'Life's Like That' letter often begins with a subordinate clause or phrase ('When . . .'/'Although . . .'); the punchline is usually a quote, though sometimes the final quote is followed by a comment.

In rewriting the example above, see how many stages you can cut from the narrative while ensuring that it remains coherent. Avoid repeating 'dilemma', used in the original to mean 'problem', and don't try to replace 'becalmed' by 'stranded', which means 'beached', or 'got stuck': the yacht didn't get stuck – it was becalmed.

Also, in compressing the narrative, beware the participle – as in 'having rescued the yacht'. First, this makes the sentence sound heavy; second, unless you're very careful, there's always a risk you'll mix up your subjects as in 'Having rescued the yacht I reminded my daughter to say thank you'. This is nonsense because 'I' didn't rescue the yacht.
Here's a rewrite of the letter:

> When my four-year-old daughter's toy yacht was becalmed in the middle of our local pond, a young man used his radio-controlled paddle steamer to bring it to the side. She was so relieved she forgot to say thank you and I had to remind her.
>
> At once she bent down and said 'Thank you very much for getting my boat for me' – to a little model sailor on the deck of the steamer.

The sub does all the work – the reader whose letter it is passes Go and collects £200.

Wynford Hicks

7
Writing headlines, etc

Writing headlines and the rest of what's called page furniture – straplines, standfirsts, crossheads, picture captions* etc – is the creative part of subbing. Lucky subs get well-written, accurate copy and have plenty of time to project it. Unlucky subs have to do their best in the circumstances.

Headline words

Headlines – especially news headlines – are written in a condensed, telegrammatic way because they have to get the reader's attention – and they have to fit the available space. All this makes for short, direct, concrete words rather than long, indirect, abstract ones: aid for assistance, bid for attempt, cut for reduce etc.

Some books on subbing advise the use of a thesaurus for headlines and even provide lists of alternative words, eg:

abandon

drop	desert
give up	drop
quit	give up
skip	leave
yield	neglect
(Gillan/Evans)	pull out
	quit
	(Hodgson)

The problem with this approach is that it tends to obscure distinctions in meaning between one word and another – without necessarily solving the sub's technical problems. So what's short for 'Abandon ship'? Is it 'Desert ship'? or

* Caption writing is discussed in Chapter 8.

'Give up ship'? or 'Neglect ship'? And how many characters are saved by this manoeuvre? One, none and none, respectively.

If precision is a general virtue in subediting, it is particularly important in headline writing. So use short, direct, concrete words wherever possible – but use them with care. Always try to use the words that convey your meaning exactly. And beware the words that have become headline-writers' clichés (see Headline clichés, p. 73).

Punctuation

There is less punctuation in page furniture than there is in text. Even if the publication's house style is to use double quotes (with single quotes inside double) for text, single quotes are always used for headlines and the rest. There is no final full stop after a headline, standfirst or caption: instead white space provides the punctuation.

Curiously some papers (eg the *Daily Mail*) retain a capital letter after a colon in headlines and captions:

Field of dreams: An aerial view of the two patterns formed in the wheat

But this practice goes against the trend and is unlikely to survive.

British headline-writing style is either caps (all words in capital letters) or upper and lower case (only the first letter and proper nouns in caps). To British eyes some American newspapers with their heavy use of initial caps in headlines look very old-fashioned:

No Disaster
For Chirac
In French
Elections

And in approach this headline (*International Herald Tribune*, 20 March 2001) looks like a contender for dullest-headline-of-the-year. Headlines should say what's happened (or happening). This one says that something (presumably expected) hasn't happened.

Quote marks in headlines

Quote marks in headlines have a vital role: they distance the publication from the opinion expressed. In the headline

Agency nurses 'a risk to patients'

the quote marks make clear that somebody other than the newspaper or magazine (in this case the Audit Commission) is making the assertion.

This practice is very important in ordinary news stories – and vital in court reports. In

Drug case doctor 'created a monster'

the quote marks make clear that the headline refers to the claim of one side in a court action.

Alliteration and other devices

Alliteration (the repetition of an initial sound) is one of the commonest devices used in headlines for light news stories and features. But there's a problem: it has its jingle effect even when nobody has intended it. The sub who wrote the following headline can't have meant to introduce a frivolous touch – but the effect is there all the same:

Speedboat kills singer as she swims with sons

And the repeated initial A in this headline makes it ridiculous:

Angry Italians, Out of the Cup, Assail Referee At Liverpool

The same point applies to puns.

Taste

There are jokes that work in the office – but not on the printed page. Take the following heading on a letters page:

Sharon and
Tracey

It links two letters – one about a Tracey, the other about a Sharon. The Tracey letter is fine: it's a light-hearted reference to the artist Tracey Emin and her Margate origins. But the Sharon one could hardly be more sombre:

> You say 'in another era . . . Ariel Sharon might have stood before a war crimes tribunal' . . . This is the era of the war crimes tribunal. The problem for humanity is that those who commit crimes against it are only tried if they lose a war.

Headline clichés

Some short words, such as axe for cancel or sack, quit for leave or resign, vow for promise, slam for criticise, shun for avoid, are headline-writers' clichés. Like all clichés they can be useful at times – but don't become dependent on them. Try to write headlines in current, colloquial English – how people actually speak – rather than tabloid jargon.

Some phrases, such as 'The British are coming' (any British success in another country) or 'Young, gifted and black' (any successful person who is young and black), are endlessly reused, then subjected to variations:

The French
are coming!

about another new wave of French films being shown in Britain.

Young, gifted and back
in England's fold

about a (white) footballer recalled to the England team.

Sports headlines are particularly cliché-ridden. If the English goalkeeper Seaman does well, he is always 'Able'; if there's uncertainty about whether Cole will play it's sure to be 'a burning question'. In rugby the British and Irish Lions are tamed (beaten) or they roar (win) – and their pride can always be called on as a third option. Cricket too inspires clumsy contrivance as in this reference to Hardy's *Far From the Madding Crowd*:

Maddy prospers far from the Test match crowd

As always, though, the worst move is not to use a cliché but to misuse it as in:

Writing on the wall for Spurs fans

This headline does not signal yet another defeat for this once-successful club – but a victory in an FA Cup match in February 2001. As all English football fans know, Spurs have often won the cup in years ending in the figure 1. Here the sub has (presumably through ignorance) reversed the meaning of 'writing on the wall'.

Variation

An important convention in headline writing is that key words used in one place cannot be repeated in another. With both the double-decker headline and the headline-plus-standfirst subs have to use their ingenuity to avoid repetition. In this feature headline-plus-standfirst the sub clearly hasn't bothered:

The internet's chastened child

Kevin O'Connor thought he could help keep the internet free of rules and regulations. Instead he brought them closer

Whereas in this strapline-plus-headline (over a story about disgraced Tory politician Jeffrey Archer) the sub has tried hard for variation – but ended up with a nonsense:

Accusations fly over funds from Kurdish charity and prime minister's attempt to get job in heritage department for his chum

Major 'wanted to make novelist a minister'

Why 'novelist' instead of 'Archer' in the main head? What's novel-writing got to do with it?

News headlines

News headlines have a double function: they attract the reader's attention and they give the gist of the story. Whereas a feature headline may intrigue, a news headline is explicit: it tells the reader what they're going to get. As well as drawing their attention to a story that may interest them, it can save them the trouble of starting to read one that probably won't.

In the old days important news stories had a series of headlines (called decks) stacked on top of each other:

TRAGIC LOSS OF TITANIC

OCEAN LINER STRUCK BY ICEBERG

MANY PASSENGERS FEARED DROWNED

Now there are two at most: a main headline with a secondary headline either above (called a strapline or overline) or below (a second deck or subhead). The main headline comes first: that is, it is almost always written first and it always contains the most important, immediate, dramatic point. It should make sense as it stands. The secondary headline provides context, explains, gives background.

Computer giant hit by global slowdown

British jobs at risk as Toshiba lays off 18,800

Israelis storm Muslim holy site

Violence erupts after protesters stone Jewish worshippers

As with the feature headline and standfirst (see below), having a subsidiary headline to explain and amplify makes it possible for the main head to be more oblique, less explicit, as in:

The fatherless baby
Lesbian couples could conceive, scientists reveal

A headline like 'The fatherless baby' – with no verb – is often called a label. Most news headlines are self-contained, stand-alone sentences – sentences because they have a verb, whether explicit or implied. They give the gist of the story as in:

Guard charged with stealing Nato secrets

Crufts judge is fined for cruelty

Cavalry officer accused of crass overtaking

Note that 'is' can be included (as in the second example) if it fits the space – but isn't essential – and that all three headlines are clear, sober and straightforward.

Light news headlines

Some news headlines need a lighter touch because the story underneath them is funny or offbeat.

Pensioner drove straight home

headlines a court story about an 87-year-old who drove his car into a wall because he'd forgotten the key to the steering lock, so couldn't steer properly.

Mr Bean saves the day as pilot loses control

introduces a story about Rowan Atkinson (who plays the accident-prone character Mr Bean) taking the controls of an aircraft when the pilot collapsed.

Although they are light in tone, both are recognisably news headlines in style because they are sentences with verbs.

Features headlines

In style and approach, features headlines are looser altogether than news headlines. They must get the reader's attention – but they do not have to be explicit. They can use word play, allusion, comment, whimsy, emotion instead of straight information. As a result subs usually have to work harder than they do with news headlines. Often it's not difficult to decide on general content: the hard part comes with finding the right words for the head – making it sing.

Take the story about scrapyard nature at the end of Chapter 5. The obvious idea is to juxtapose a word like nature or wildlife with scrap or scrapyard. But a combination of these general words won't work as well as an example. As with writing features, so with writing headlines for them: the specific instance described in vivid detail works best.

Something like SWALLOWS IN THE SCRAP or BLACKBIRD ON A BICYCLE is more effective than SCRAPYARD WILDLIFE, while BUNNIES IN THE OVEN is brilliant but unpublishable. SCRAPMAN AND ROBIN (written by a pre-entry journalism student) is difficult to beat.

A feature on the Victorian painter Landseer included three key points: he specialised in painting animals; he was Queen Victoria's favourite painter; he was commissioned to paint her dogs. The headline VICTORIA'S PET PAINTER brought the three points together neatly.

Features headlines and standfirsts

Most features headlines are combined with a standfirst – and a picture. Here's a typical example (the picture shows Tom Green and his five wives):

Tom Green stands in a Utah dock today facing a possible 25 years in prison for polygamy. Duncan Campbell visits the family encampment to hear a tale of forbidden love

Meet the wife – all five of them

The headline takes a familiar phrase and gives it a new twist. The standfirst is the classic two-sentence version: the first sentence explains what the story's all about and says why you're reading it now; the second sentence, which incorporates the byline (Duncan Campbell), gives more detail on the feature itself.

The standfirst can be extended if there is more space or more to say – but generally the two-sentence version works better than longer ones. The second sentence can be cut to a simple 'Duncan Campbell reports', or the standfirst can be cut to a single sentence: 'Duncan Campbell talks to the family of a man facing a possible 25 years in prison for polygamy'.

Letter heads

Headlines on the letters page can be sober and straightforward or show a lighter touch. Where a letter expresses opinion the headline can summarise it without having to use quote marks since the context makes clear that the views expressed are not the paper's.

Time to tax the fat cats

tells the reader what to expect.

Letters based on good jokes are a challenge to the sub. Here's one, published in the *Times* on 1 December 2000, with its headline:

2b, or possibly 2a

Sir, Given the National Trust's apparent confusion over precisely in which house Shakespeare's mother lived (report, November 30), surely the correct response is to put a plaque on both their houses?

Breakers: crossheads, sideheads, pull quotes, drop caps . . .

There are various devices intended to break up a page of text so that it looks more interesting and is easier to read. For example, the crosshead is a line or lines taken from the text (the next par or two), set bigger and bolder than the body copy and inserted between paragraphs. It is centred and the paragraph that follows is indented in the usual way.

This is a crosshead

The sidehead, by contrast, is set flush left.

This is a sidehead
The paragraph that follows is also set flush left. The sidehead functions as a mini-headline and is generally used to start a new section.

Unfortunately, some newspaper and magazine designers treat the two devices as interchangeable – which is confusing for subeditors and readers alike.

Pull quotes are taken from the text, set bigger and bolder than the body copy and displayed on the page as a taster for the story. They are not placed between paragraphs but dropped into the text so that the reader reads across them;

> **'This is a pull quote, set bigger and bolder than the body copy'**

they are sometimes set across more than one column and usually ruled off, as here. They are often edited – shortened and simplified – but it is essential that their meaning should not be changed.

The drop (or sometimes raised) cap is often used to start stories and as a visual breaker on the page. There are several points to watch out for. First, the paragraph following the drop must be long enough to go below it.

Second, be careful of the sequence of drop caps on the page – avoid repeating the same letter. Third, it's always awkward to combine drop caps and quotes. Either you go for a quote mark that matches the original cap:

'**B**ut this looks silly because at first glance the quote doesn't seem to end. Or you go for a quote mark taken from the body copy:

'**B**ut this one looks like a pimple. Or you leave the quote mark out altogether hoping nobody will notice: this looks, and is, illiterate.

If a drop cap is essential here there's no solution to the problem except to rewrite the paragraph so that it doesn't start with a quote.

Extras: boxes, tables, graphs, maps, diagrams . . .

The simplest extra that can be added to a feature is an address with phone number and other details so the reader can contact the organisation mentioned. There is nothing more irritating for a reader than having to hunt down a phone number when it could have been provided. Boxes, panels and side-bars (all names for the same thing) can include simple or complex facts, large quantities of information, statistics, advice, even comment (for examples see the features chapter of *Writing for Journalists*, pp. 86–90).

In general these extras and their visual equivalent – graphs, maps and diagrams – are planned as an integral part of the feature rather than being added in at the subbing stage. But subs need to be on the lookout for opportunities to make a feature work better. This might be by adding an element that is missing or by taking a section out of the main feature and boxing it.

Bills and coverlines

Newspaper subs write bills, the posters that you see on news-stands promoting the particular edition of a paper. Here the trick is to attract the readers attention and arouse their interest without fully satisfying their curiosity. (The purpose of a bill, after all, is to get them to buy the paper.) If the story concerns a famous person, they will not be named; if an important decision has been made it will not be given; and so on. In style, too, bills differ from news headlines in that they are more likely to be labels, less likely to have a verb.

The story about Rowan Atkinson headlined 'MR BEAN SAVES THE DAY AS PILOT LOSES CONTROL' might be promoted as

TV STAR IN
MID-AIR
RESCUE

The headline 'BRITISH JOBS AT RISK AS TOSHIBA LAYS OFF 18,800' as a bill would become much more general, something like:

THREAT TO
BRITISH
COMPUTER JOBS

Magazine subs generally write coverlines. But on some magazines they are seen as too important to be left to the subs so they are written by lofty people called executive editors. It can go higher than that: Felix Dennis, founder and boss of Dennis Publishing, says that the best part of his job is working on the coverlines for *Maxim*.

Essentially coverlines sell the magazine: they entice the reader into buying. They must be legible, from a distance and among the competition: this is an important part of the persuasion to buy. It's a good exercise to stand in a newsagent and see which covers work and think about why they work.

One or more of them must promise a clear benefit to the reader – a sound reason to buy – and/or offer something to new readers, somewhere to begin, a way in to whatever the subject matter is. One leading magazine publisher has a list of hot words and phrases for coverlines: new, now, today, discover, know, learn, help, rated, best, worst, we show, quick, essential, how to, complete, better, easy, guaranteed . . . and many more.

Here are some classics from *Cosmopolitan* in its heyday:

**Those funny foolish
things that
passion makes us do**

**Naked ambition – will he
jilt you for his job?**

Why aren't you
getting promoted?
Maybe it's your
personality

On the same cover as these, however, was:

Sleepless nights?
We'll teach you
tricks to slumber

'Slumber'? As a variation on 'sleep' this just doesn't work. 'Tricks to slumber' is worse than clumsy.

And then there was this:

What it really
means when he says
says *I love you*

Yes, that's right: the word 'says' appears twice. Which goes to show that flair is never enough: attention to detail and careful proofreading remain essential.

Wynford Hicks

8

Checking pictures and writing captions

Checking pictures

Look carefully at the four pictures on pp. 84–5. Can you spot anything wrong with them?

How many errors did you find? (See p. 94 for the answers.)

Whether or not subs do layout they must check pictures – photographs, drawings, maps, diagrams – as well as copy before writing captions. Is the picture accurate? Are the people/objects in it what they are supposed to be?

Flipping is a common source of confusion. The most celebrated case was Billy the Kid, shown as left-handed in a classic early photograph, much reproduced in newspapers then and now, and the source of the myth that he was left-handed. But according to Ian Mayes, writing in the *Guardian*, the technique used at that time (1880) automatically reversed the image. For once, newspaper production staff were not to blame for the confusion. (For a full account see Appendix 2, p. 169.)

Posed pictures are always dangerous. To follow Fergie on p. 85, here's one where the mistake emerges only when you check the picture against the accompanying text (see Figure 8.5, p. 86). According to the text Yasmin works in Birmingham and is reunited with Robin at Euston – whereas the photo shows two models posing at Waterloo (then served by NetworkSouthEast).

Subs must be on the lookout for conflict between pictures and copy. Are we using an old pic of a bald actor with an interviewer's up-to-date observation of his 'distinguished grey hair' (actually a wig)? Perhaps writer and photographer have gone to see the interviewee at different times – and seen different things.

Having been interviewed people often tidy themselves up for the photographer – which is fine except where the writer makes a point of the dishevelled state they were in beforehand. Here's an example. The intro reads: 'Tie wildly askew

(8.1)

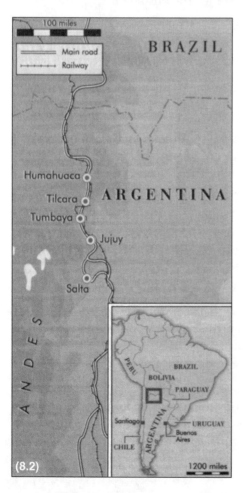

(8.2)

(8.3)

Figures 8.1–8.4

(8.4)

Figure 8.5 'Every Friday evening Yasmin Archer leaves her Birmingham
office in time to catch the 6.45pm train to Euston'

and collar undone, sporting a hairstyle that can best be described as exuberant, Terry Humphreys looks like a man who need answer for his appearance to no one.'

But the picture (Figure 8.6) shows a neatly tied tie and a perfectly buttoned shirt (even if the hairstyle is a bit exuberant). Collapse of intro – egg on sub's face. To state the obvious, this kind of thing is not the writer's or the photographer's fault.

It's the sub's job to see that the different elements of copy, pictures, captions and other page furniture support and complement, rather than undermine, each other. For this to happen the sub who writes a caption must read the accompanying copy – and look at the picture. Sounds obvious and simple, doesn't it? But it clearly didn't happen in the following examples.

The picture (Figure 8.7) shows the England cricket captain Nasser Hussain in the nets having played a disastrous front-foot shot – behind him his middle stump has been knocked out of the ground. Instead of some joky reference to his poor form or this not being exactly good for morale, the caption starts with an awful cliché and carries on as though the sub has seen only half the picture.

Figure 8.6 'Tie wildly askew and collar undone, sporting a hairstyle that can best be described as exuberant, Terry Humphreys looks like a man who need answer for his appearance to no one'

Figure 8.7 'Captain's innings: Hussain goes on the front foot during England's net practice in Faisalabad yesterday in preparation for the second Test'

Source: Picture Laurence Griffiths/All Sport

A story headlined 'Shadows over Elena's life in the sun' has the sombre strapline 'The murdered millionaire's widow who is ready to fight a bitter battle'. But the pictures are upbeat to say the least. One shows Elena positively gambolling in the surf with her new husband – the sunniest of smiles on her face. The caption reads: 'Lonely lady: Elena is unhappy despite the love of husband Tim.' Well, she may be but that is not what the picture shows.

A caption can be accurate – but at the same time misleading or ridiculous if it conflicts with the picture. The caption that read 'Out of their element: Two white rhinos at Whipsnade Zoo pondering the continuing cold weather yesterday' was presumably accurate – they were technically 'white' rhinos. But it was ridiculous because the point of the picture was the snow in the background: seen against snow the rhino looked the opposite of white. (If this was intended to be funny, it didn't work.)

Some pictures defy the caption-writer – unless they are licensed to write a joky caption. If a businessman falls asleep at the top table you can hardly caption the resulting picture 'Michael Gifford, chief executive, says the surprise rights issue will help Rank in its intention to expand in the leisure industry'. But that doesn't stop some people.

Over the page by contrast is the snap of a sleeping person turned into a front-page splash with Fergie making the picture by turning round to look at Ted Heath (Figure 8.8). Note also that the closed eyes of Fergie's neighbour are explained – if they weren't the reader would naturally assume that he was asleep too. If the camera lies, the caption should say so.

A sub must write a caption for the picture the reader is actually going to see. To do this they must see the picture after it has been cropped in case important detail is lost. Here are two examples of bad cropping, both from the *Guardian*. The first appears as a correction: 'The picture illustrating our report about a crop mark in the shape of a seven-pointed star, page 7, yesterday, puzzled some readers who could only count six points. It was (no pun intended) the way it was cropped. A wider view would have provided the extra point.'

The second is shown on p. 91.

The caption says 'two of the 75,000 plus revellers' – but alas the accurate figure, according to the picture (Figure 8.9), is one and a half.

Subs must also know how the picture will reproduce. A black labrador that's clearly visible on a large black-and-white print may disappear into the dark background when the picture appears in the paper. So the caption should not

COURT

SSHH.. TED'S HAVING A ZZZ

NAPPING!

Ted Heath had a quiet snooze after lunch yesterday – in the royal box at Wimbledon.

Everyone pretended not to notice as the former Tory premier rumbled gently through the afternoon ... except for the Duchess of York.

Fergie, who expects her baby in five weeks, turned round and giggled openly as Ted slept on, oblivious to the roars of the 16,000 fans as Sweden's Stefan Edberg trounced Czech Miloslav Mecir.

Buzzer Hadingham, tournament chairman who has spent Wimbledon fortnight calming the players' tempers, was wide awake on Fergie's left – except for a blink when the camera clicked.

The tennis-loving duchess chatted all through the game, sustained by £150 boxes of chocolates which she munched. But tired Ted, needless to say, didn't get any.

Figure 8.8

Figure 8.9   'Leading the way . . . two of the 75,000 plus revellers in Leeds'

Source: © The *Guardian*

include incidental detail if there's a risk of it disappearing. (If, on the other hand, the disappearing detail is important, you can use an arrow or other device to identify it.)

Then there's the question of colour, which we can't illustrate here. But it's essential that you know how colour pictures will be seen by the reader, before you write your caption. Otherwise you risk calling things green when they look brown and vice versa.

Lastly, even if subs don't do the page layout they should check it. Otherwise they may find pictures turning up in the wrong places. If a page layout has two picture slots of the same size, sod's law rules that the two pictures will be transposed.

Writing captions

A caption has two functions: it identifies key elements in the picture and it's a side door into the story – the reader's attention is caught by the pic and held by an intriguing caption. Then they start to read the story.

Just as captions shouldn't contradict pictures so they shouldn't irritatingly tell you what you can see for yourself. Instead, they should answer the questions you would ask. It follows that appropriate captions for a picture vary from one publication to another: general readers will need things explained that specialist readers already know.

The first element in a caption is often a mini-headline, or kicker, eg in the examples quoted above, 'Captain's innings', 'Lonely lady' and 'Out of their element'. A colon (or sometimes three dots) then leads on to the information part of the caption. Learn this basic caption-writing style first.

The style has a number of variants. With portraits the mini-headline is often followed by a simple identification: 'Lonely lady: Elena.' Or the two elements can be reversed: 'Elena Nugent: lonely lady.' Or the identification can be followed by a condensed quote: 'Elena Nugent: "terribly helpless".' These formulas are clearly more effective than the simple name caption 'Elena Nugent' – but try to avoid cliché.

A constraint here is that headline phrases used elsewhere on the page can't be repeated in the caption (see p. 74).

A caption can of course be much longer – it can be extended into a self-contained picture story. The Fergie–Ted Heath story is one of these. Note that it begins with the main point of the picture.

If several pictures are chosen as a sequence – or are linked in any way – the caption writer's job is to point up the connection, say, by a series of mini-headlines 'Bewitched . . .', 'Bothered . . .', 'Bewildered . . .'.

Usually the caption is based on material contained in the story. But it may consist of material cut from it for reasons of space. Never forget that the object is to bring the reader into the story so even with this kind of caption try to suggest a link.

Like words, pictures are read from left to right. If there is any chance of confusion, identify explicitly: from left, left, centre etc.

The conventional place for a caption is underneath the picture: that is where readers expect to find it. Sometimes page designers like to give a page of pictures a single caption; in this case words like 'top left' and 'clockwise' are needed to identify individual pictures.

Captions have their own clichés: people 'share' jokes when two or more of them are snapped smiling at each other; they're described as 'receiving' or 'being awarded' medals and certificates when they're clearly posing after getting them; they 'find time to relax' when they're sitting in an armchair. Avoid these formulas where possible.

Tenses are a problem in captions. It's obvious that the present tenses are generally preferable to the past ones – they emphasise that you are looking at something happening. But what do you do if you have to add a past element to a present caption? Don't, whatever you do, mix the two up in one sentence: 'The Queen presents a medal as she reviewed the troops yesterday' is as bad as any other clash of tenses – and more prominent than most. If you have to use both present and past tenses in the same caption, at least divide them into separate sentences.

The plain verb form 'presents' is almost always better than the participle 'presenting' used by some amateurish caption writers. The plain form is simpler and more direct. As always accuracy is the main thing. Is it Ann or Anne? Is that a rifle or a shotgun? Is that the mayor or their deputy? If you want to avoid embarrassing mistakes, check.

And beware of making things up. A sub once changed 'Strolling in the park' to 'Mother and daughter stroll in the park', which cost the paper a few bob when aunty sued. 'Romantic couple' is another lawyers' retirement fund contributor – with the help of incensed brothers and sisters.

Cautionary tale

Photographer Ronan Quinlan wrote this in the *Journalist's* Chief sub column:

> I once photographed a man with his wife and another woman for an evening newspaper social column. It was a boring must-be-done picture at a boring must-be-done function. I knew the people: the woman on the left was the wife and the caption said so. It said so in print, but the picture showed her in the middle.
>
> The editor intuitively understood the problem – the photographer had goofed. I scrutinised the picture. It was not reversed, manipulated, cut, collated or otherwise mutilated. The caption was exactly as I had written it. I concluded with a rare acknowledgement – the editor was right.
>
> But so was I. For a colleague working for the daily paper in the group had shot the same three people in a different order, and the pictures had fallen victim to a three-card trick on the desk, his picture appearing with my caption.
>
> It was the desk's fault, but for the editor, instant justification: TWO photographers had goofed.
>
> Next time you have a snag with a caption, try this solution: ask the photographer. He or she may just be right.

Answers (for p. 83)

In picture one (Figure 8.1) the illustrator has given the octopus nine instead of eight tentacles; in two (Figure 8.2), the maps contradict each other (the detailed one is wrong – Bolivia appears as Brazil); in three (Figure 8.3), the 40-year-old Prince Charles has been flipped (printed the wrong way round – look at his wristwatch and buttonhole); in four (Figure 8.4), an obviously posed picture of Fergie and her family 'playing Monopoly', a hotel appears on Park Lane with not even a house on Mayfair (this is not allowed in the game).

Wynford Hicks

9
Proofreading

In an ideal world, by the time a piece of work reaches proof stage there should be nothing to correct. A well-organised editorial system will have ensured that the hard work of knocking copy into shape, correcting factual errors and improving spelling and grammar has been done while the words were still in manuscript, whether that was digital or paper.

Copy which still requires significant alterations during proofreading indicates an editorial process which is slack, indecisive, disorganised, unprofessional or some permutation of all four characteristics. If major work at this stage becomes habitual (the occasional panic change for last-minute reasons can be considered endemic to journalistic publishing), seek a remedy further up the production chain.

Proofreading should, therefore, be undertaken with the aim of changing as little as possible. The reasons for this are obvious, no matter where proofing comes in the production process.

On a newspaper which lays out pages using unsubbed copy, proofing will be one of the final stages, likely to come at a time when pressure is mounting and time is at a premium. Mistakes which are not picked up first time round will increase the pressure further – if they are picked up at all.

On a magazine which sets type before doing layouts, giving uncorrected material to the art department is a pointless and costly waste of time, even when using an in-house typographic system. The set copy cannot be used for layouts because it may be shortened (or lengthened) and making corrections to an already set piece of work increases the chances of introducing further mistakes.

In the days when typesetting was done outside the office, in either the compositors' department or a contracted repro house, this really would have been expensive because the more times a piece went to and fro, the more charges were levied. Even with in-house, or in-office, facilities it is a good idea to stick to the old disciplines, not for the sake of tradition but because they can save time and improve accuracy. Employing people to do work which will have to be done again is never a good idea, and it's a wasteful use of computer facilities.

Since we do not live in an ideal word, however, proofreading is still a necessary stage in the subediting process. In fact it is probably more necessary than ever as fewer and fewer eyes see a piece of work on its way from copy to published article. The way in which proofing work is arranged will vary from office to office but there are certain principles to adhere to.

The first thing to remember is that proofreading is not an innate ability, but an acquired skill. Anyone can become a good proofreader though many can't be bothered to concentrate hard enough. A while ago the following 'test' came around as a round-robin email:

> Count the number of Fs in the following text: finished files are the result of years of scientific study combined with the experience of years. [Answer at end of chapter.]

Most people, apparently, count wrongly on their first try. The reason given in the message was, 'The brain cannot process the Fs in "of"'. Clearly this is nonsense; if the brain could not process the F in 'of', the word 'of' would not exist. A longer but more accurate explanation would be that most people rush over the text and don't pay any attention to the smallest words. The art of accurate proofreading lies in paying attention to every word, long or small – and then in knowing how to make corrections. If you can train yourself to do this then you will have acquired a valuable skill.

Festina lente

Put the term 'proofreading' into an internet search engine and you will turn up hundreds of leads which fall into two main categories. One comprises the commercial organisations which offer a proofreading service; the other, more interestingly in this context, the 'writing labs' of American universities which offer online advice to students about how to improve their essays and term papers.

Most of them offer similar advice, but this paragraph, published by Virginia Tech though originally from the University of Maryland, summarises the necessity of reading carefully:

> when you read normally, you often see only the shells of words – the first and last few letters, perhaps. You 'fix your eyes' on the print only

three or four times per line, or less. You take in the words between your
fixation points with your peripheral vision, which gets less accurate the
farther it is from the point. The average reader can only take in six letters
accurately with one fixation. This means you have to fix your eyes on
almost every word you have written and do it twice in longer words, in
order to proofread accurately. You have to look at the word, not slide
over it.

Other tips these sites offer are to read aloud (perhaps not a popular strategy
in a busy office), to use a cover such as a sheet of paper or a ruler to encourage
a line-by-line review, to proofread in tandem with someone else, and even to
read backwards from the end.

Does advice intended for students hold good for subeditors working to deadline? In principle, yes, it does. It is possible to proofread quickly but impossible
to proofread in a rush. As outlined above, the trick is to make yourself read
– not skim, not glance. Word-recognition habits make it easy to overlook little
words like 'of' but also to miss extra letters buried in words like asssess, efffec-
tive, agggregate. Use a ruler – or covering sheet of paper – to go through the
proof line by line, word by word, letter by letter.

Sharing the task is another possibility which should be considered. The editorial training manual of one major publishing house specifies: 'Always have at
least two people proofread every page (not including any specialists who may
have to approve pages).' This is probably something to be wished for rather
than accepted as regular practice, but if accuracy is important then it is worth
trying. When two or more people share the task, make sure that everyone
reads the same proof, so that it is clear what corrections have already been
picked up.

Making the right mark

Corrections should be indicated using the proper proofing symbols, which are
specified in British Standard BS 5261: Part 2: 1976. This system replaced the
earlier BS 1219: 1958. Anyone who started working before 1976 will have
learnt the earlier set of marks, and both systems are still in use. There are
many similarities between the two, but the 1976 system does away with the
use of English words or abbreviations in favour of what is intended to be an
internationally recognisable set of marks.

Thus, for instance, when a word or letter has to be changed to bold type a
wavy line is made underneath the relevant text and where the 1958 system
requires the word 'bold' in the margin, the 1976 system repeats the wavy
line. Perhaps the most persistent hangover from the past is the symbol used

to indicate a space. It used to be a hash sign which could be used on its own to mean 'add more space' or augmented by the words 'less' or 'eq' (meaning equalise the space). Now it is a mark which looks like an umbrella which has been blown inside out (for more) or the right way up (for less). In any event, the new system is easy enough to learn and the advice should be to adopt it. If, however, your office still uses the old system, you must abide by that.

Marks should be made clearly and confidently. The purpose of correction is to show someone else exactly what and where the mistake is so they can correct it; if they have to pore over your scrawled or faintly inked marks it will waste time and may lead to further errors.

There is also a system of colour coding associated with the proof-correction symbols which allows the mistake to be attributed and thus, if necessary, charged to the correct account. The typesetter's corrector (if there is one) should mark any mistakes made during composition in green; the subeditor should mark any mistakes made by the typesetter in red, and any other alterations or corrections in blue or black. (All this is explained very clearly in the British Standards Institution's publication BS 5261C: 1976, available from the BSI. A new 50-page booklet on this subject was in preparation at the time of writing. Check www.bsi-global.com/group.xhtml for current details.)

Where typesetting is still an external function (that is to say, not carried out by the subeditor who has handled the copy or is doing the proofing) it is necessary to compare the proof with the original copy in order to attribute errors. This is one area where digital copy and desktop publishing can, in theory, cut down on time and mistakes. If the copy is subedited thoroughly there is no reason why spurious errors should be introduced, although the manual addition of bold or italic emphases still leaves scope for cutting words or spaces.

Typographical proofing

There is more to proofreading than simply checking for spelling mistakes. Just as copy should be written according to the house style (or subedited to conform), so typesetting must be checked for conformity to the design style. Is the piece set in the right size of the right fount on the right leading (line spacing)? Have the house rules on use of bold or italic been followed? If you are proofing a laid-out page, does it have the correct specifications for head-lines, standfirsts, captions and other page furniture? Are there indents where there should be and are they of the right depth? If the publication uses drop caps, are they present and correct?

These are the large-scale checks which should be easy to make if you follow the house-style guide (and if there isn't one, either badger the chief sub or art editor into compiling one or compile your own).

With the big elements checked and out of the way you can attend to the minutiae of proofreading – word spacing, letter spacing and widows. With the first two of these you are essentially looking for gaps which are too big or too small. Sometimes an automated typesetting system will create a line in which there are enormous gaps between the letters or the words (or both), and you must know how to make it look better. The exact details will depend on the software in use, but it would be universal to check the tracking (space between characters), horizontal alignment (especially for a 'forced' setting) and H & J (hyphenation and justification).

Widow is the term used to describe a word on its own in a line and it should be a matter of professional pride to make sure there are no single-word lines in anything you have proofread.There are several ways to solve the problem – subbing a word or words in or out, or adjusting the tracking to 'squeeze' the line of type, though this should never be taken to noticeable extremes, which generally means a reduction of no more than minus five.

When proofing page layouts, the conscientious subeditor should also check for running turns. This is a matter of making sure that columns of type do not start or end with paragraph breaks. To put it another way, the paragraph must run over the turn, including the turn at the end of a page (unless it is the last page, of course). The reasoning behind this is that a break might encourage the reader to stop reading. Some magazines even insist that a page does not end with a full stop in case the reader takes it as the end of the article.

For anyone serious about improving their knowledge of typography and type-setting it is worthwhile reading some of the classic texts, such as *Hart's Rules for Compositors and Readers at the University Press, Oxford*, S. H. Steinberg's *Five Hundred Years of Printing* or *Handling Newspaper Text* by Harold Evans.

Kind cuts

Even on the best-organised publication, there will be times when the subeditor has to make drastic alterations to a proof at the last minute. It may be that a more important news item has to be fitted into the page or perhaps the adver-tising department has sold space which must come out of editorial.

At moments like this you have to be bold and decisive. It's no good tinkering about with individual words in sentences. Cut whole sentences and if possible whole paragraphs, and make cuts which the typesetter (or designer or even yourself if you're doing the layout) will find easy to make without fiddling around – the less fiddling, the lower the likelihood of mistakes.

Of course you must do your best to keep faith with the author, and the piece must still make sense so you can't simply slash. It is also a good idea to keep the original copy either as a digital file or on paper just in case your decisions are disputed after the fact; in fact keeping files and revisions of files is good practice generally and you should either abide by the office system, get whoever is in charge to implement a system if there isn't one or, failing that, devise and keep your own.

Answer (How many Fs?, p. 96)

There are six Fs. 'Anyone who counts all six on the first go is a genius – three is normal, four quite rare,' according to the original message.

Tim Holmes

10

Legal and ethical problems for subeditors

This book is not about the law or ethics but those topics are of such importance to journalism that no book about subediting would be complete without considering them. That said, a single chapter should not be considered a replacement for a full-length book such as *McNae's Essential Law for Journalists* or, best of all, a proper training course run by an accredited organisation.

The subeditor is in a position of great, and probably increasing, importance when it comes to legal and ethical matters. 'Subs are the last line of defence,' according to Jessany Marsden, editorial training manager at IPC Media. Her colleague Peter Genower (editor-in-chief of *TV Times* and chairman of the Periodicals Training Council's training committee) reinforced her opinion by observing that knowledge of the law had become much more important in an age when people – and readers – have become more litigious and more aware of their rights.

This is not news. In their 1998 book *Magazine Law: A Practical Guide*, Peter Mason and Derrick Smith wrote: 'Subeditors must have an even sharper knowledge than writers of the laws that influence what magazines can and cannot publish.' The same applies to newspapers, but websites face further difficulties. Because they are 'published' internationally, they may be subject to different interpretations of the law: this is discussed further in Chapter 13.

The subeditor should not, however, be acting alone. Every publication should have access to a lawyer's opinion, both before publishing something which may be contentious and after receiving a complaint, threat of action or writ following publication.

In practice, newspapers are more likely to call upon this service frequently but it should be noted that any periodical, even the most obscure hobby magazine, can find itself on the wrong end of a legal action. The sub should therefore know what to do and who to call on in case of doubt. As the chief subeditor of Trinity Mirror's paper the *Wharf* observed: 'If you have a legal question, go to the lawyers instantly. It's not your job to make things legally sound – it's your job to recognise when a story needs a legal opinion.'

However, even the most expert legal opinion is no guarantee of protection. Colin Myler, former editor of the *Sunday Mirror*, discovered this in April 2001 when his paper published an interview with the father of an alleged assault victim while the case was still in progress (it is discussed further below). A sub with even the most rudimentary knowledge of the law should have had the phrase 'contempt of court' going off like an alarm clock, but editors have a habit of pushing at the boundaries of what is acceptable, and this story was run after legal advice had been taken.

A subeditor can get a publication into trouble passively, by not picking up a dubious statement in a piece of copy, or actively, by changing copy so that it becomes defamatory, by attaching a libellous headline or standfirst to the copy, or by captioning a picture badly. A photograph can, in itself, be libellous. Coverlines on a magazine can also lead to trouble, as can poor punctuation. Even if all of the above are legally sound, there may be questions of ethics surrounding them.

Law

A subeditor should at the very minimum have a working knowledge of the laws governing defamation, malicious falsehoods and copyright. A fully trained sub, and certainly anyone dealing with news, must also know about the absolute or qualified privilege of reporting courts, tribunals, company meetings and government (local, regional and national), contempt of court and trademarks.

Defamation: unwarranted badmouthing as understood by Joe Public

The legal systems of the UK are based on case law, that is, on how judges interpret the statutes, and those interpretations can change or evolve over time. As a result there is no single, absolute definition of what constitutes a defamatory statement but a commonly acknowledged starting point is this ruling made in 1840: 'A publication . . . which is calculated to injure the reputation of another by exposing him to hatred, contempt or ridicule.'

Subsequent judgments have added that a defamatory statement is one which may cause a person to be shunned or avoided; disparages a person in their office, profession or trade; tends to make right-thinking people think less of a person.

'Right-thinking people', a term for which there is also no definition, in practice means the members of the jury who hear a case for defamation. Whatever has been published, it must be understood by these people, who are assumed to have no special knowledge of the subject matter, to be defamatory. As *McNae's* explains: 'It is not the meaning intended by the person who wrote the words, nor indeed the meaning given to them by the person to whom they were published.' Although this makes it practically impossible to decide how a 'right-thinking person' would interpret any given words, Mason and Smith suggest trying to predict how the publication's readers would react.

At the same time, the law (in its concrete expression as pronouncements by judges over the years) recognises that a free press must be allowed to report wrongdoing and that such reports may damage the reputations of individuals. The key point is that such reports must be accurate, fair, justified – and provable.

Subeditors cannot be expected to research stories and, as the old phrase has it, stand them up, but they must know when a story may be defamatory. Subs should also be aware that injudicious copy editing may cause a story to become defamatory, particularly if the fairness and balance are affected, or if evidence which justifies the claims being made against a person is cut.

Defamation can take the form of libel or slander. A libel is a defamatory statement which is published in permanent form (such as print or broadcast journalism), whereas a slander is spoken. Libel is therefore the most prevalent concern, although journalists (in interviews or even in phone conversations) may lay themselves open to charges of slander.

Inept use of a photograph may also be defamatory. The news editor of a top-selling weekly title recalled 'a man being circled in a photo as the paedophile referred to in the story – wrong guy was circled, lawsuit, big money paid out'. That's a fairly obvious example, but subs responsible for layout should also beware the perils of juxtaposing the innocent and the guilty: running a big picture of a local worthy next to a headline which screams 'My sex-change hell' might just be funny – but it might just be defamatory, too.

Think twice about reusing photos commissioned for one story to illustrate another. The person who posed for a heartwarming tale of selfless charity might not care to be used to stand for something less salubrious. Mason and Smith cite a library picture of a lorry being used to illustrate a story about the mistreatment of livestock in transport: wrong lorry shown, wrong company clearly identified in the signwriting, wrong side of the law.

And if a photo can do it, so can a caption. The weekly's news editor again: 'Another story was about swingers and we had to run a panel of people's comments next to it. One was a guy who ran swinging nights at a club but he was labelled by subs in the caption as "committed swinger" – he wasn't and threatened to sue.'

Finally, note that the humble comma can be a powerful force for good or evil. Used incorrectly it can make an apparently innocuous sentence into a costly libel. Indeed punctuation can completely change the meaning of a sentence. To illustrate the point have a go at punctuating this old chestnut: 'Woman without her man is nothing.' (Answer at end of chapter.)

Malicious falsehoods: knocking copy

Pushed for space and up against a deadline, a subeditor working on the *Scotsman*'s TV listings cut four words in the description of a programme and inserted three others. The copy now fitted perfectly.

Unfortunately the words he used altered the meaning of the description, so that the show changed from a tribute to a singer 'who was struck down by a brain tumour last year' to one 'who died of a brain tumour last year'. The singer had not died and was understandably upset. Had he been sufficiently upset to believe that the change was made deliberately and with the intention of harming his earnings, he could have sued for malicious falsehood.

Like many words used in a legal context, 'malice' carries more meaning than its general usage. Certainly it refers to spite and ill-will but journalists who publish something they know to be untrue, or which they have been told is untrue, or who don't care whether it is true or not, are held to be acting maliciously. If untrue information is published for personal gain or some other dishonest motive then that is a malicious falsehood.

Again, there is not much a subeditor can do about the origination of potentially malicious copy but it should be considered a duty to catch it before publication. This will probably require some checking back with the writer or editor. Pay particular attention to reviews of products or services; a critical review or test is not in itself malicious but harsh and negative comments may be used as the basis for an action. These four guidelines should see you safe:

- always test the product according to the manufacturer's instructions for use
- if conducting a comparison test, make sure you compare like with like
- have evidence of the accuracy of your facts
- always give the manufacturer the opportunity of responding to poor results before publication.

The subeditor does have the power to make matters worse by presenting critical copy in a way which draws special attention to it. A sensational headline in huge type or an unwarrantedly prominent position on the page might be used as evidence of malice.

Copyright: whose line is it anyway?

It is unlikely that a subeditor will run much risk of falling foul of the copyright laws as far as copy is concerned. Unless you deliberately insert great chunks of copyright material (novels, plays, song lyrics, film dialogue, other journalism etc), most quotes will come under the heading of 'fair dealing'. You may use other people's words in a report of current events or in a review, provided that the source is acknowledged and that they do not form a 'substantial part' of the copy. How much is a 'substantial part'? There is no legal definition, but if it is enough to lower the commercial value of the work in question then the author might have a claim for infringement of copyright and for damages.

Pictures are what the subeditor should beware of. Before using any picture or photograph – including those which arrive with press releases – you should check that your publication has the right to use it. Even if it comes out of the library (be that physical or digital) because it has been used before, it may be that copyright reverted to the creator after the first use. Although it is not uncommon for newspapers to 'grab' pictures from broadcast material, this is not legally condoned and such material should be acknowledged and paid for.

Iain White, editor of *Playstation 2: Greatest Hits*, came across the following unexpected problem with pictures when he was putting together the launch issue. It's the kind of thing that a subeditor can expect to get extra brownie points for knowing about:

> We had a top 50 DVD review section with images supplied from other magazines our company published. My senior art director advised me that I could only use images that were for films 'currently in promotion'. I checked and this only covered one image. We borrowed the 50 movies in DVD format from a local retailer and screen-grabbed the images ourselves that night. We were legally in the clear to do so as this counts as 'editorial comment'. Problem solved, another day in court averted.

Perhaps the reporter has persuaded someone to take a photograph from their photo album to illustrate a piece about a family member in the news. If the picture was taken by a commercial photographer, it is likely that the copyright remains with them, especially if the picture was taken after the Copyright Designs and Patents Act 1988 came into force.

The reverse of this is where a commercial photographer (who has retained the copyright) offers your publication a picture of someone in the news. There is no copyright problem here but there may be an infringement of the family's right to privacy; the person who commissioned the picture usually controls the right to distribution even if they don't own the copyright.

Subs working for local newspapers, news agencies and magazines specialising in human interest stories should pay particular attention to the use of pictures for these reasons. Those employed on celebrity magazines should note the increasing tendency to litigation by stars and near-stars who feel their privacy – or exclusivity – has been invaded. In July 2001 the Press Complaints Commission rejected a claim by Anna Ford that pictures which the *Daily Mail* and *OK!* had published, of her on a public beach, invaded her privacy. Ford applied to the high court for a judicial review of the ruling but her challenge was not allowed.

Michael Douglas and Catherine Zeta-Jones, on the other hand, were able to obtain an injunction in November 2000 against *Hello!* magazine publishing photographs from their wedding – the rights to cover it had been sold to *OK!*

The interesting legal point is that both actions were based on the European Convention on Human Rights, which was incorporated into English law in 2000. The relevant clauses in the convention have not yet been tested in court (that is, no precedent has been established to form the basis of future rulings), so this is an area in which subeditors must keep up to date, even if it is likely to be the editor who decides to run pictures such as these. It is also possible that the convention may affect the interpretation of freedom of expression in cases of defamation.

The way a picture is cropped can also lead to trouble. When three newspapers ran pictures of J. K. Rowling, author of the Harry Potter books, on a beach in Mauritius she decided not to complain. *OK!* used the same picture but did not crop out Rowling's eight-year-old daughter and the PCC upheld the author's complaint that the magazine had breached the rule that children must not be interviewed or photographed without the consent of a parent.

Privilege and qualified privilege: the right to report

Even in these days of small staffs it is unlikely that the person who reports court or other quasi-legal proceedings will be the same person who subedits the copy. The prime responsibility for submitting a report which will not get the publication into hot water must rest with the reporter. Nevertheless the subeditor must have a keen awareness of what can and cannot be published and the form which such reports should take. Where there is a small staff, court reports might be submitted by an inexperienced freelance or by a news agency reporter who could be a student on work experience. In such cases, the subeditor really is the last line of defence. And don't think that if you work on a magazine this doesn't apply to you: all sorts of magazines, business and consumer, use court-based copy or run features based on or around court cases or tribunals.

In a nutshell, the press is allowed to give a full and fair report of proceedings in court without being open to an action for defamation, even if what was said in court was defamatory. This right, known as privilege, was established by the Law of Libel Amendment Act 1888, which stated: 'A fair and accurate report in any newspaper of proceedings publicly heard before any court exercising judicial authority shall, if published contemporaneously with such proceedings, be privileged.' The Defamation Act of 1996 confirmed this and made it clear that the privilege is absolute, that is, it is not open to challenge.

Provided, that is, the report meets the criteria specified below.

It must be fair – both sides in the case must be treated equally. This does not mean that each must be allocated the same number of words in the report, but that allegations and rebuttals must be reported fully. A subeditor cutting copy must therefore be careful to maintain that balance. Allegations must not be reported as fact, and must be attributed to the person who made them.

It must be accurate – the facts must be correct. Did the defendant plead guilty or not guilty – and to what charge? Was the defendant acquitted or convicted – and of what charge? If these are not reported correctly then an action for defamation could be brought. It goes without saying that names, ages and addresses must be correct.

It must be published contemporaneously – that is, in the very next issue of the newspaper or magazine. A morning paper will carry the previous day's cases, an evening paper those from the morning or previous afternoon, a weekly those from the previous week.

Proceedings must be in public – most are, but evidence which is heard 'in camera' cannot be reported, nor can evidence ruled inadmissible.

It must be the 'proceedings' of the court which are reported – comments from the public gallery are not covered by privilege, nor are interviews with people somehow connected with the trial, like a police officer, a lawyer or a relation of the defendant.

The sub should be particularly careful to ensure that headlines and intros connected with court reports are 'fair and accurate'. Watch out for headlines based on sensational allegations: until they have been proved to be true or false they remain allegations and readers must understand them to be such. Page furniture can be just as defamatory as copy.

Court reporting is the only situation to attract absolute privilege, but newspapers and magazines can claim qualified privilege when reporting on international organisations and courts, courts martial, tribunals, parliamentary and local government proceedings, company meetings and on the 'finding and decision' of a public or trade association (see the Schedule to the 1952 Defamation Act for the full definitions).

Privilege in these circumstances is 'qualified' not because it affords less protection but because a judge must decide on whether any published item comes within this legal protection. The item must not only be fair and accurate, it must also be published without malice and in the public interest. As Mason and Smith phrase it: 'The person making the communication has an interest or a duty – legal, social or moral – to make it to someone who has a corresponding interest in it. This reciprocity is essential.'

Comments made outside the circumstances defined in the Schedule are not covered, so beware of follow-up quotes or interviews.

Contempt of court: speaking out of turn

It is a widely quoted axiom that in English law a person is innocent until proved guilty. This principle provides a rough and ready guide to the boundaries of contempt: is this material likely to sway a juror's mind or otherwise prejudge the outcome of the trial? However, it is impossible to give a clear cut definition of what will or will not be judged to be in contempt of court. The *Sunday Mirror*'s legal advisers thought that an interview with Muhammad Najeib published on 8 April 2001 was OK. The judge presiding over the trial of Leeds footballers Jonathan Woodgate and Lee Bowyer (and two of Woodgate's friends) thought otherwise. His opinion was that the interview would prejudice the case, in which the four were accused of beating Sarfraz Najeib, Muhammad's son. The jury was discharged and the trial halted. The paper's editor, Colin Myler, resigned, and the attorney general decided to apply for contempt proceedings against the publisher, Trinity Mirror.

This was not a subediting problem; the decision to run the piece was taken at the highest level, and the editor paid the price. It is, however, illustrative of the kind of problem which a subeditor can help to avoid. Contempt of court can arise from a simple error, such as reporting that someone has committed a crime rather than that they have been accused of committing it, or disclosing an accused person's previous convictions, or even publishing a picture of the accused if identification is to be an issue in the trial. It can also arise from publishing interviews with witnesses or, as we have seen, relations.

The Contempt of Court Act 1981 establishes when and how a person or publication may be in contempt and every subeditor should know the main clauses off by heart.

Trade names: Hoovering up Sellotape

It is not a crime to use a registered trade name without capitalising the first letter, or to use a specific name in a generic sense. It is, however, poor subediting and if the company or its lawyers spot such a use you can expect a letter demanding that in future the name is used correctly. In effect, the registration of a trade name gives its owner copyright protection and if it is not defended the owner can lose the exclusive right to its use.

This can affect journalists and advertising personnel. Some years ago a newly established motorcycle manufacturer bought the rights to a very old-established and well-known marque name which had been in limbo for some time. The marque logo had been adopted by many different companies without redress; it was found on T-shirts, mugs, advertisements for spare parts and so on. The new owner's first course of action was to contact everyone discovered to be using the logo, telling them to cease and desist – including magazines running copy which made reference to the (unauthorised) use and advertisements which depicted the logo or name.

A subeditor must be aware of trade names and registered brands and use the correct spelling and punctuation. For example, the well-known British cross-country vehicle was a Land-Rover but is now a Land Rover while its more sophisticated sister has always been a Range Rover. An American might dress a wound with a Band-Aid when a British person would prefer Elastoplast.

Pay particular attention to trade names which have become generics. It seems quite natural to use Hoover when we mean vacuum cleaner and Sellotape when we mean transparent sticky tape but making the specific stand for the general is inaccurate and unprofessional. Persistent misuse might lead to a lawyer's letter or even a civil suit.

What, though, of the four-letter word used for both unwanted email and pork luncheon meat? Describing it as a generic use seems wrong, and the capital letter makes an essential distinction. This is the kind of question which might form the basis of a lively discussion on the Fleet Street Forum website (http://www.honk.co.uk/fleetstreet/forum.htm).

Letters: the dangers of green ink

A subeditor in charge of the publication's letters page should not make the mistake of thinking that a reader's letter cannot be defamatory. If it contains defamatory statements and you publish it, it is subject to exactly the same laws as any other published material and your publication could be put in the position of having to prove the writer's claims to be true. Always check the accuracy of facts stated in letters, especially if a controversial view is being put forward.

Subs should also be careful about cutting letters (see p. 65). The balance of a writer's argument, or the overall meaning, must not be substantially altered.

A letter may also contravene the Public Order Act of 1986 if it is likely to arouse racial hatred.

There is, of course, much more to the law as it affects journalists and it should be stressed again that this chapter is no substitute for a proper training course.

Ethics

If the law defines what a newspaper, magazine or website may safely publish without running the risk of being taken to court, journalists' ethical codes help them to make decisions that will keep their consciences clear and allow them to sleep soundly. In other words, just because you can legally get away with saying something about someone which may hurt or damage them doesn't mean that you should do so. That makes it sound easy and clearcut, but in the fast-moving, messy, commercial world of journalism, knowing the right thing to do and making sure it's done are two different things, and decisions may be affected by a range of external factors.

Every journalists' organisation which has ever existed has devised a code of conduct. In the UK, the National Union of Journalists and the Institute of Journalists have codes, and you can examine the NUJ's at www.nuj.org.uk. If you would like to put this in a wider context, look at the Ethicnet site; here the University of Tampere in Finland has amassed the codes of journalist organisations from all round the world, together with academic papers about the ethics of journalism: www.uta.fi/ethicnet/ethicnet.html.

British publications also operate under the code of practice formulated by the Press Complaints Commission. As the PCC is a self-regulatory body, neither the code nor the PCC's judgments have the force of law, but most publications observe the former and abide by the latter if they transgress. The PCC's site, which includes the code and much else is at www.pcc.org.uk.

These codes are all well and good if you think that the world is a black-and-white kind of place, but there are many shades of grey. What is the ethical situation when a sensitively written piece about a difficult subject is undermined by a subeditor's joky or insensitive headline or coverline? 'I did a story about a bus driver who cheated on his wife,' a feature writer for a women's weekly recalls. 'The woman was happy with her story but not at all happy with the sub's headline "The driver on the bus goes bonk, bonk, bonk". She thought it belittled her sad tale. Another headline was "www.cheatingsod.com" about a woman whose husband left her for an internet lover. These things happened every week and I often felt uncomfortable.'

Ethical issues of a different sort are raised when companies or organisations publish their own magazines (or have them published by a third party). Sometimes this might be a consumer matter such as pushing the company's

---

The subeditor on a medical magazine published by a major professional organisation comments:

'We have sometimes been put under pressure to compromise our editorial independence if we are reporting something which shows the organisation in an unfavourable light. As subs we have to get copy refereed by specialists within the organisation. So if I'm subbing a feature on organ donation, I have to email it to the ethics department so they can check it for factual errors. Most of these referees understand that we are journalists and don't try to tamper with the copy – but not all. I have had more than a few heated discussions with people who want to change quotes, rewrite passages etc. Ninety-five per cent of the time I get my way but on a few occasions I haven't. I once had the head of the organisation on the phone telling me to spike an article by a well-known writer. In the end we kept it but pulled another article so we could have the head replying on the facing page. It looked absolutely ridiculous and lord knows what people thought about it, but we had no choice if we wanted to keep our jobs.'

product when a different product is known to be better, but if the organisation is concerned with politics, the law or medicine it could be a matter with more philosophical weight behind it. In this situation a subeditor could find him- or herself trying to defend the freedom of the press.

Law and ethics: specific subediting issues

Subeditors should be particularly aware of the following points:

- Juxtaposition – make sure that layouts do not juxtapose elements which may lead to a picture or story becoming defamatory.

- Malicious falsehood – if you're going to say someone's dead, make sure they are; if a product test is negative, make sure you can stand up the findings.

- Subbing court reports – must be fair and accurate for absolute privilege. Headlines and introductory matter must not exaggerate.

- Contempt of court – nothing in the report must be capable of prejudicing the outcome of a trial, and that includes pictures.

- Defamatory pictures – when using library shots to illustrate a story make sure there's nothing defamatory to the subject depicted.

- Headlines – legally, they can be defamatory, as can standfirsts, captions and other page furniture; ethically, think about the overall effect. If your clever headline undermines a sensitively written story, is it worth using?

- Punctuation – can lead to trouble if used incorrectly.

Answer (punctuation riddle, p. 104)

An English professor wrote the words, 'Woman without her man is nothing' on the blackboard and directed the students to punctuate it correctly.

The men wrote: 'Woman, without her man, is nothing.'

The women wrote: 'Woman! Without her, man is nothing.'

Tim Holmes

11

Understanding production

The photograph for the front cover has disappeared, the computer files containing a major story are lost in a database, you don't know where you are in the countdown to deadline, you're about to miss your slot on the printing press, your publication will certainly lose sales, it's all your fault and you could lose your job. But not before you have had a very expensive photographer on the phone asking for his valuable transparencies back, an irate contributor wanting to know who inserted several gross inaccuracies in her copy, the printer's production controller nagging you to deliver material according to schedule, and an editor or publisher (or both) raving at you for all of the above and more.

Sounds messy, doesn't it? Luckily, it can all be avoided by following the simple tried and tested guidelines for production outlined in this chapter.

Newspapers, magazines and websites are living, changing entities. Michael Barnard puts it very well in *Magazine & Journal Production* when he says:

> There are few business activities where, when the end result of commercial enterprise is a saleable product, that product is essentially different every time it is produced . . . publishing is one of them.

Material flows in, around and out all the time; people will be working on the current issue, planning and commissioning forthcoming issues and, we hope, archiving previous issues. On a daily paper this will be happening relentlessly, at a speed dictated by daily schedules and with a large number of people to mislay items.

If a major story – such as the terrorist attack on New York – breaks, your task will be intensified enormously. Writing about the *Times*'s newsroom on the afternoon of 11 September 2001, Brian MacArthur noted:

> By 4.30pm, the *Times* had planned 30 pages on the story, the schedule listed 40 different story lines and *Times 2* had changed its cover story and was already printing. Now at least 50,000 words had to be written

and subbed, pictures chosen and pages designed, all within three hours (which didn't quite happen).

Weeklies have more time but not always as much as you might think. Analysing American press reaction to the events of that dreadful Tuesday, Robert Paget wrote in the *Observer*:

> *Time* and *Newsweek* were fortunate. With their Friday publication dates, they had time to work on the background and analysis but the poor weekly *New York Observer* was not so lucky. It publishes on Wednesdays and had only a few hours to scramble for a story, and remake its edition.

Fortnightlies and monthlies do have the time but usually fewer people to do what has to be done. Websites which carry breaking news may be updating by the minute. There is plenty of scope on any publication for material to get lost, misnamed, misfiled and mistreated and more often than not it falls to a subeditor to prevent these disasters. In short, you need to be organised.

With luck the operation you work for already has an efficient production system in place. Established newspapers will almost certainly have a set of routines to cover what happens before, during and after production. Make sure you get trained in how to use them.

Many magazines, even some published by larger companies, have a surprisingly slapdash approach to training and handing over legacies. Perhaps they have never quite got round to systematising their procedures, or everything might have been in the head of the person who has just left. Whatever the situation, a good subeditor must take on board the rules which do exist, follow them and be prepared to consider ways of improving them.

Just think about the material required for the simplest of stories or features – copy, page furniture, and probably at least one picture. Each of these is likely to come in from a different source, be combined on the page and then dispersed to different storage areas. Multiply this by the number of stories on a page or features in a magazine, complicate it by having pictures sourced from different photographers or picture libraries, by having two or more writers working on the copy, by publishing different issues and by passing everything through a number of pairs of hands and the scale of the potential for chaos becomes evident.

Organisation becomes all the more important when material is coming from, going to, or being stored in, a central computer server. If you misfile hard copy or a printed photograph, painstaking searching through in trays, desk drawers and filing cabinets may – but not always – reveal its whereabouts; misfile something on a server and you not only have to deal with the screening power of technology, you also have to find one file in a database which may contain thousands of files, probably identified by cryptic names which offer little clue as to their content. Do you want to be the one who has to open them one by one until you find what's missing?

So, begin at the beginning. It would be helpful to have a book with 'Don't Panic' on the cover in big, friendly letters but the next best thing is a production manual which you can make for yourself. Start off by taking stock. If there is even a vestigial system for doing things, sketch out how it works and who is responsible for what. If you are a new bug in an established organisation remember that there are people there who have built up this way of working for any number of reasons and any or all of them might have a vested interest in things staying as they are. Those people include the editor, freelance contributors, staff writers, production colleagues and sales staff.

If you want a true picture of your publication, never forget the sales staff. You are working in a commercial nexus and your newspaper, magazine or website (unless it's a BBC site) needs advertising to survive. The higher you go in the production chain, the more important the advertising side will become to your planning and scheduling so don't fall into the trap of dismissing ad people as an irrelevant nuisance. Apart from anything else you might want their co-operation and goodwill when a big story comes in and you need to shift things around. When the World Trade towers were attacked, 'The *Scotsman* completely changed its format, wiping advertisements from the first 12 pages', as Jean Morgan reported in *Press Gazette*. It was far from the only paper to take such action.

Newspapers and magazines tend to have production systems which work in different ways, but just as important is the distinction between a large organisation which allocates specialised roles and a small one which expects individuals to tackle a variety of tasks. Underlying all this is the truth that a good production process needs to be based on some simple administrative tools. One of the most important is the job description – if you don't know what you are meant to be doing, you can't do it. If you know but your colleagues don't, you will spend your time explaining, arguing, duplicating effort, overlooking omissions and sorting out other people's mistakes. So rule one for every production system must be to make sure that everyone knows what to do, when, and how to do it.

The second rule must be a well-planned hierarchy of folders and files for the editorial computer system. A suite of software like Quark Publishing System is almost infinitely customisable when it comes to setting up folders, access privileges and status (a way of showing what stage a piece of work has reached); the temptation to complicate must be strongly resisted. As with so many other things in life, the acronym KISS should be your mantra – Keep It Simple,

Stupid. At the most basic level there need to be folders for unsubbed copy, subbed copy, pictures or artwork, finished pages, though these can obviously have different names or even be assigned to a job description (chief sub, art editor).

QPS can be configured to prevent certain classes of employee getting access to certain folders. For example, all subeditors might have access to the unsubbed copy folder but once they have sent their work to the subbed copy folder, only the chief sub can get at it. In practice, installers of QPS have noticed that whatever the original intentions, most systems are eventually configured in a fairly 'flat' way, with relatively few exclusive privileges.

Once the hierarchy of the computer system, classes of folders, access privileges, statuses and so on have been set up, subeditors must make sure they take files from the right place and send them to the right place, with the right status. This is where even a modicum of training is so important. Although most systems are fairly easy to use, they are not always intuitive, especially when it comes to learning the folder/file/status nomenclature. Considering that forgetting to change one item on a drop-down menu might send a piece of work careering off in the wrong direction, a properly structured induction process is not only essential but also cost effective. Any organisation which does not do this is not just asking for trouble: it will rapidly find itself in trouble.

Newspaper

It is becoming increasingly difficult to describe a 'standard' newspaper production procedure. Ripples from the de-demarcation caused by the collapse of union power are still spreading, and this is combined with working on computer systems which encourage a rather different way of doing things from the long-established formulas. Some papers are divided into self-contained sections (news, features, sport etc), each having writers, subs and layout subs; some have a 'flat' production system in which all subs work on all sections; some have 'modularised' systems where a small collective works on a particular page from start to finish.

There are, however, still enough similarities to sketch in a day's work. Although what follows may not be 'typical', it is based on the reality of a major regional daily. It should be read in conjunction with Will Ham Bevan's description of his work as a newspaper sub in Chapter 2.

The production process starts with the flatplan. This comes up from the planning department first thing in the morning and shows how many pages the paper will have that day, what advertisements have been booked, which pages they will be appearing on and where on the page.

The flatplan is taken to the first editorial conference, attended by the editor or deputy editor and section heads, where decisions are made about which stories to follow, their relative importance, how much space to allow them, whether they warrant any subsidiary elements such as background sidebars or explanatory graphics. This will be written up as the schedule, a list which assigns writers to stories and so on. It would be unusual for a subeditor to be involved at this stage but on a small newspaper the chief sub might be included.

In the afternoon a second conference will firm up the editorial content and look over pages which have been designed already. Then in the early evening there is a handover meeting at which the night team will be briefed.

After first conference the copy and pictures will start to flow, reporters sending them to the appropriate folder or basket (to use the traditional newspaper term). There may be a protocol for naming a file, or the system itself may impose certain elements of the file name, but it should certainly indicate the paper, the date, the section, something to identify the story and, if necessary, the edition.

By now, whoever is responsible for deciding what goes where on which page (possibly the page editor on a new-look regional or local, probably the chief sub on a small weekly, usually the night editor on a daily's news pages) will be working up a plan for each page, the result of which is called the scheme (Figure 11.1). Then the elements of each page scheme are gathered together and listed on a check sheet which specifies:

- the date
- the page number
- whether it is a colour page or not
- what the lead story on the page is
- its length
- whether it has pictures
- whether it is part of a package (and what the other elements are)
- whether it is hard or electronic copy
- other stories on the page (with sub-divisions listing length, pix etc).

The sheet and any physical copy or pictures are put into a tray, from which they are picked up by the designers to be fashioned into pages. A first proof of each page, which may be nothing more than a skeletal outline of the major elements, will be printed off and attached to the production record. The

FOR DESIGN

DATE:

PAGE:

COLOUR?

YES/NO

	● NAME	● NUMBER	● SIZE	● PIX?
● LEAD STORY				

● IS IT A PACKAGE????? WITH WHAT?		● BRIEFS??	

● PICTURE WITH LEAD? ELECTRONIC/HARD COPY		● NOTES	

OTHER STORIES ON PAGE

	● NAME	● NUMBER	● SIZE	● PIX?	● NOTES
1:					
2:					
3:					
4:					
5:					
6:					
7:					
8:					
9:					

Figure 11.1 Newspaper scheme

second proof is likely to include the copy and pictures, with dummy headlines and other page furniture and, after being printed for the record, this is passed to the subs for attention to copy and display type.

Neither designers nor subs should be tempted to use dummy page furniture of an obscene nature. It is surprising what can be overlooked as the pressure mounts, and while it is embarrassing enough to let a page slip through with something like '84pt headline here please' instead of 'PM heads war cabinet' it could be personally and corporately costly to omit to change '84pt f**k b*ll*cks sh*t b*gg*r'.

A real, if mild, example of this is captured in the *Guardian*'s book of *Corrections and Clarifications*:

> A caption in *Guardian Weekend*, page 102, November 13, read 'Binch of crappy travel mags'. That should, of course, have been 'bunch'. But more to the point it should not have been there at all. It was a dummy which we failed to replace with the real caption. It was not meant to be a comment on perfectly good travel brochures. Apologies.
>
> (17 November 1999)

Although nothing can legislate against such human weakness, heavy-duty production systems like QPS can at least ensure that accidental damage is restricted. Whereas a sub working on a stand-alone version of Quark would have to go into the layout itself to change the copy, the publishing system can and should be set up to ensure that subeditors have full access to all the words (body copy and associated elements such as headline, standfirst, captions) but cannot change the basic geometry (ie layout) of the page. Quark does this through its Copy Desk programme, and other brands will have similar arrangements.

A new proof with subbed copy and complete page furniture will be printed off for the production record and the page passed on to the chief sub or night editor to pass or send back for revision. When it has been OKed for the last time the complete page is saved as an Encapsulated PostScript (EPS) file, and sent off to be made into printer's pairs; that is to say, juxtaposed with other pages so that everything is printed in the right order. Advertisements are stripped in by a special piece of software and the stories on each page are archived automatically.

Our case-study paper got the first pages (Arts) to the designers at 1.30pm. The subs received them at 2pm and had until 7pm to get them passed. The last two pages (Sports, naturally) went to design at 10pm, to the subs by 10.30 and were offscreen by 11.10, ready for the presses to roll.

Magazine

When you're hiking in the mountains and the mist comes down it's always a good idea to have a map and a compass. The flatplan is a map of the magazine and the way it's used, is the compass. It will be drawn up at the beginning of the production cycle and it will show how the content, both editorial and advertising, is to be arranged throughout the book. (Planning a magazine is a skill in itself and although it is not your immediate concern as a subeditor, it is worth learning about; John Morrish covers the topic very well in his book *Magazine Editing*.)

A flatplan can consist of anything from a list on a single page of A4 via a schema of outlined oblongs representing pages to a special board into which page proofs or reduced-size photocopies of pages can be slotted. Perhaps a combination is best – everyone should have a single sheet to show what's in the issue, but it makes more sense to have a centralised flatplan on the office wall to track production, kept up to date by a designated person (probably the chief sub). This should also help to reveal problems in good time so that, if necessary, to continue the metaphor with which we started, you can break out the torch, whistle and emergency rations.

Whatever form it takes, the flatplan should be able to record what stage every page is at. On the other hand it should not be too complicated, so it could just show what has been commissioned, written, laid out, proofed and sent to the printer. It must also show the page's location in the computerised production system.

No matter how sophisticated the production process of your title, forget the idea of a paperless office. Nothing beats the simplicity of a piece of paper and an envelope to keep tabs on material. The piece of paper we can call a top sheet (Figure 11.2) and the envelope (which could be a polythene zip lock item) a job bag; together they are like the baton in a relay race to be handed over to, and on by, whoever is working on the document. The top sheet should be a form which records:

- the title of the magazine
- the issue the job is scheduled for
- the author's name and contact details
- the file name given to the copy (see p. 122)
- where the document is in the production system
- who has worked on it.

57 March To PDF: Fri Jan 12	Feature name:							
Section:	Writer:							
Page numbers								

Document version	Date	Location

Notes/please tick	Before sending …

Text	
Tech edit	
Pix	
Captions	
Subbed	
Spell check and word count	
Printed proof	
Ready to send	

Figure 11.2 Magazine top sheet

These last two points will vary according to any individual publication's working methods, but a typical form might include categories for Raw Copy, Subbed Copy, To Art, To Production, Back to Art, Final Check and To Print.

The job bag must be big enough to include a hard copy printout of the original story, subsequent subbed versions, and any artwork which has not been digitised (photographic prints, transparencies, illustrations).

This leads logically to the next point – naming digital files. Working within the hierarchy of the computerised system, files should be named to reflect:

- the name and issue of the publication
- the topic of the copy
- the version of the file
- the initials of the last person to work on the file.

Let us imagine a magazine called *British Bike*. You are working on issue 45, subbing a piece of copy about Triumph Bonnevilles. The filename might look like BB45.Bonny.2.th:

BB45 (name, issue, never changes)

Bonny (copy tag, never changes)

2 (second electronic version of the file, changes whenever the file is altered)

th (initials of the last person to work on the file, changes whenever someone works on it).

It is also worth noting that some editorial programs, among them Quark Copy Desk and Atex, have a function which allows the person working on a piece of copy to make 'invisible' notes for the next person in the chain. Invisible in this context means that they will show up on the screen but not on a proof. Using this facility a subeditor can make changes but also leave the original for instant comparison.

Commissioning

Another aspect of production worth knowing about is commissioning – the act of requesting material from a contributor, be it words or pictures. This is not strictly a subeditor's responsibility, although in many publications it will come within the remit of the production section. Whoever the responsibility falls to, if it goes wrong it will be the subeditors who have to work longer and harder to make things right or get production back on track. Clear and accurate commissioning can save many headaches, notably subbing problems and production delays.

The act of commissioning is also a devolution of power – you are putting part of the future of the publication into the hands of an outsider. It is essential that the right person is chosen for the job, whether the desired result is words, photographs or an illustration. This does not necessarily mean following an entirely conventional path. For example, the novelist Ian McEwan, whose rate of production must normally be relatively slow, was able to provide the *Guardian* with 1,000 words at two hours' notice for the rapidly rejigged issue of 12 September 2001.

On the whole, however, a daily newspaper or weekly periodical should commission those who understand the need for quick delivery, whereas a monthly or quarterly magazine which can plan ahead will be able to choose people who need a bit longer. This need for certainty about quality and reliability explains why certain freelances are used over and over again and why it is so difficult for a newcomer to join their ranks. Trust must be earned, and there is a major chicken-and-egg riddle here.

Whoever is chosen for the job must be given a comprehensive (which does not mean long) brief. This should specify:

- the subject
- the angle or approach
- the length
- the deadline
- specific aspects which should be covered
- areas which should not be covered
- extras required (sidebars, photographs, illustrations)
- delivery format (hard copy, disk, email, PDF)
- the rights you are purchasing (single use, worldwide, digital as well as print etc)
- the fee.

You might also want to include ideas about possible interviewees and suggestions for background or research.

If the commission is for photographs or an illustration, details should include:

- mono, colour or both
- prints or transparencies (unless it's all digital)
- particular points to emphasise or cover
- special requirements – for example, a photo to be used on the cover must be a certain shape, have room to include the masthead, tasters, bar code etc.

Once the material has been commissioned, it is essential that progress be monitored. This does not mean the commissioned person should be harassed but regular (and constructive) communication is a good idea. Make it clear that you can and should be contacted if any problems arise and that you won't just blow your top – which does not mean that you can never blow your top, only that you won't do it every time!

When the material has been delivered it must be assessed. If it is unacceptable the ideal solution is to return it with clear instructions as to where it falls short. However, pressures of time may mean that it has to be salvaged in-house, with a rewrite (if it's words) or a rapid revision of the layout to accommodate different photos or illustrations.

Filing lark

In every old-fashioned but well-organised publishing house, there will be a dusty-looking person whose sole function is to maintain a library of everything which has been published. Or, in these downsized times, such a service may be contracted out to a specialist firm. Or the editorial system will run this routine automatically.

But, if you are really unlucky, you may have to do the archiving yourself. Not long ago this might have meant turning the job bag into an archive bag, removing everything which had to be sent back to the author or photographer, and putting what was left into a filing cabinet. The good news, however, is that many publishers have realised that this material has a commercial value and organise its compilation onto searchable CD-ROMs – so it becomes someone else's job. It is also possible to transfer the digital files for an issue onto another hard drive or onto CDs, although simple transfers are unlikely to have the same benefits of searchability as a proper archiving set-up.

Never forget

No matter how hard you strive for seamless production, the thing to remember about any system is that it is not perfectible. A combination of human failings (cussedness, personality clashes), hardware which is still relatively fragile (computer crashes), software which is never bug free (programme freezes) and time which is not expandable (deadlines) means that occasionally something will go wrong. You have to be flexible, you have to be prepared to work the extra hours and you have to make compromises. If this seems to fly in the face of your determination to make everything go right, all the time, every time, bear in mind Michael Barnard's wise words:

> The successful production person is he who achieves the compromise least unacceptable to most people. If, additionally, some of his colleagues also believe he is assisting, rather than impeding, the creative process, he is doing well indeed.

Tim Holmes

12
Publishing technology

If you ever find yourself in the mid-Wales market town of Brecon, take a trip to the county museum. There, halfway up the stairs to the third floor, you'll find a slide show and if you wait for a while you will be treated to a short film.

It was shot, by an amateur, in 1992 and shows the last edition of the *Brecon & Radnor Express* to be produced at its old printing works. You will see scenes which, apart from details of clothing and haircuts, could have come from any time in the preceding century. Lino men sit at hot-metal typesetting machines, keying in copy from scrappy sheets of paper, coaxing the slugs of type to line up properly; a time hand working on the stone puts together a complete page of type in a metal-cased forme, knocks it into shape (literally, with a mallet), screws it down and then hefts it off to the foundry. We don't see the next stage, but a papier mâché impression of the page would have been taken and used as a mould for the printing plate. The cameraman does show us the plate being fixed to the printing press and inked up before the presses roll for the last time.

It's fascinating if you have any feeling for the romance of old-fashioned news-paper making, and that's the point – it was old-fashioned by provincial newspaper standards, but not as old-fashioned as you might think. Many local paper publishers had slung out the massive, messy hot-metal Linotypes by the 1980s and switched to computerised photo-typesetting, but as late as 1985 national dailies as diverse as the *Financial Times* and the *Sun* were still set in hot metal.

Photocomposition did away with the old machines but kept, more or less, the manning levels and hierarchies of the unionised compositors' room. The keyboard operator output the words onto photosensitive paper instead of lines of lead and the time hands put down their mallets and took up scalpels and gum to cut and paste layouts (including the halftones for pictures) on special grid sheets. The completed paste-up was put under a process camera, and a printing plate photo-etched from the resulting sheet of film.

As far as national newspapers were concerned, the new era was set in progress by a freesheet in Warrington owned by Eddie Shah. In a nutshell, Shah took on the printing unions by refusing to recognise the usual closed shop arrangement by which only union members could perform production operations. With backing from the editor of the *Sunday Times*, Andrew Neil, the Cheshire police and the Greater Manchester force's anti-riot Tactical Aid Group, a large and unruly union demonstration was routed in the early hours of 29 November 1983.

Shah's Messenger group papers were put together in the usual photocomposition, cut-and-paste way but the standard book on the subject, Goodhart and Wintour's *Eddie Shah and the Newspaper Revolution*, contains this telling passage:

> During and after the dispute the papers were being set . . . by four young women straight out of secretarial college who had been trained . . . for only two weeks. Several experienced craftsmen with four-year apprenticeships behind them could no doubt have done a better job, but not that much better, and would have cost the employer a good deal more.

If those young women could do such a good job, surely journalists could too. The next step was for Shah to found the UK's first national newspaper to be produced by journalists inputting copy directly to the computerised system and made up by subeditors (not compositors) working on screen. *Today* was launched in March 1986. Other new papers followed, of which the *Independent* and *Sunday Sport* have survived longest.

The reason for outlining the move towards electronic production is because it was such an important event, for journalists as well as managers. Printing and publishing had been, for various reasons, constrained by rules and regulations enforced by a variety of trade unions, so what should have been simple industrial progress – the introduction of new machinery – became a series of momentous events which literally made the headlines. When the *Reading Evening Post* became the first paper in the UK to move from hot-metal typesetting to photocomposition in 1965 so much was made of it that no one in the district could fail to know what had happened.

As a result of these events, the subeditor's job changed radically and for ever. Previously: 'Every activity concerning the production of a national newspaper after the article, headline or photograph left the hands of the journalist was strictly controlled by a member of one of the unions who jealously and dogmatically guarded their long standing monopolistic position,' as Michael Crozier put it in his book *The Making of the Independent*. (Photographers were also affected – they were not allowed to develop, print or wire their own pictures.) Now a sub can, indeed must, deal with all of those things right the way through the production process, only finishing when the page is made into a plate and the presses start to roll.

For publishers the changes meant more efficient staffing arrangements, no more closed shop and, of course, reduced costs. The capital investment required for new computers and software was, in some cases, recouped in a year.

Partly as a result of Eddie Shah's actions, several regional newspaper groups were able to make rapid progress with direct input but Shah was by no means the first newspaper owner who wanted to move to newer production technology. In the 1970s the *Daily Mirror*, the *Financial Times* and the *Times* had all tried and failed to adopt processes which were common in American papers. *Today* is an important factor, however, because it was the first national paper to succeed in installing a fully electronic production system operated by non-print labour (or even non-unionised labour). Shah blazed the trail for Rupert Murdoch's Wapping site and Murdoch opened the floodgates for everyone. Suddenly, it seemed, anyone who could afford a computer and the relevant software could start a newspaper or magazine. The author of this chapter did just that, setting up with a not-quite-bottom-of-the-range Amstrad and a version of Ventura Publisher.

Tempting as it is to see the march of progress as a by-product of the march of technology or the result of one man's crusade, the end for the time-warped procedures of print production came about for the usual combination of reasons – technological advances which provided cheaper alternatives, social and economic changes, and political will. Desktop publishing (DTP) hardware and software, the laws enacted by the Conservative government to restrict trade union strike action, and a social consensus which approved of those laws swept away the lot.

To understand the possibilities opened up by the introduction of direct input and complete electronic page make-up you only have to look at the many books about DTP published immediately after *Today*'s launch. One lists seven different types of computer (not makes, types, each with a different operating system), another describes 14 different software packages. As far as professional work was concerned this soon boiled down to two types of system and a handful of programs. Major publishing organisations would opt for a large-scale, multiuser, database-driven system centred on a mainframe with numbers of 'client' terminals of the kind which had been developed in the United States. Smaller operations could buy one or more personal computers (both Apple Macintosh and IBM PC) and load them with off-the-shelf software.

Today was kitted out with a Hastech system. Shah had seen this in action on American papers published by the Gannett group – but he had not seen the complete picture. Goodhart and Wintour claimed that he was 'leapfrogging at least two stages in the evolution of British newspapers'. Sometimes, however, it is better to follow a pioneer rather than be one. In a retrospective piece published in August 1996 *Printing World* noted:

> Installation problems and the capacity of the Hastech system dogged the paper from the beginning. The full pagination system had been seen running at a Gannett centre outside New York City; however, at another Gannett site, the capacity problem had led the papers to install an alarm system with flashing red lights. When it started up, journalists had to delete as many unnecessary files as possible to keep the system from crashing. For *Today*, transmission times were also a problem and with delays in pagination, deadlines had to be brought further forward until sports coverage was seriously affected.

Eddie Shah later admitted that the paper had been plagued with technological problems causing setbacks from which it never recovered. Everything Shah tried to do – direct input, journalists on stories sending copy by modem, on-screen page make-up, fully integrated colour scanning, satellite transmission to remote printing sites, straight to plate printing – is now standard practice, but the technology he chose was not quite up to the job.

The upside of computerisation for journalists and particularly subeditors was instant control over setting and laying out copy. No more making corrections, sending them back to the comps who could and would, on a bad day, introduce more errors, making more corrections, sending them back, and so on. Now the sub could call up the copy on a screen, make the corrections there and then, print out a clean galley proof. It is true to say that *Today* ushered in a new era of newspaper and magazine production, free from the restrictions and demarcations imposed by printing craft unions. It also involved added responsibility, usually for little or no extra money, and the requirement for subs to command new design and technological skills. Whatever the rights and wrongs of union customs, skilled compositors knew how to produce good typesetting, something which now falls to the subeditor. One of the chief requirements of a good sub is to operate effectively whichever computerised system is installed.

Even in 1986 there were competing systems on offer. Eddie Shah did not have to opt for Hastech and some commentators feel his choice was an example of inexperience mixed with a quixotic nature. The founders of the next national paper to be launched made the very rational decision to go to what was then the biggest supplier of typesetting equipment in the world, and thus it was that the *Independent* was launched in October 1986 on an Atex system.

Atex was, and in some people's opinion still is, the heavyweight of the news publishing world. This system had at its heart a mainframe server, to which individual workstations could be networked. It could cope with copy input, news agency wires, subediting, page layout and the integration of graphics. From the start, the *Independent* was praised for its layouts and the use of pictures but none of this happened just as a result of using computerised production; Crozier's book reveals the long hours which went into deciding on a look and then formatting the computer to recreate it. At the other end of the publishing scale, Rupert Murdoch had chosen Atex to equip the Wapping site for his four national newspapers. This turned out to be very useful for the *Independent* as the many *Times* and *Sunday Times* journalists it recruited had valuable experience of the system.

Current Atex systems integrate established programmes like Microsoft Word, QuarkXPress and Adobe InDesign into a customised database which structures copy flow, pagination, archiving and a host of other features.

This is very similar to Quark's own Quark Publishing System (QPS), which incorporates the company's layout software with a special word processor called Copy Desk and runs both through a custom-built database to create a comprehensive package which has found great favour among magazine publishers. Like every professional system QPS can be configured to give different degrees of access to different grades of journalist and offers control over every aspect of production, from showing story length through hyphenation and justification to micro-control over tracking and leading.

In truth, there are a number of companies offering packages which all work in a very similar fashion. In fact, after industry commentator David M. Cole attended several product demonstrations at the NEXPO 2001 publishing fair, he was moved to say: 'It's all the same . . . I believe that all the major suppliers meet their competitors, feature for feature, in the major categories.' Exhibitors included Advanced Technical Solutions, Geac Publishing Systems, MerlinOne, Advanced Publishing Technology, Harris Publishing Systems, Baseview Products and Mactive. They all use a central database to run the system, they all use PCs or Macs as 'intelligent' terminals rather than the 'dumb' proprietary units of the 1980s, and they all integrate proprietary software from companies like Microsoft, Lotus, Quark and Adobe.

Europe also has a couple of major players in this market. Net-linx AG of Germany acquired established companies Ctext, SII and Computext to bolster its position and now offers systems for directory, newspaper and web publishing. CCI Europe's Newsdesk system, produced in Denmark, operates in the way described above, with every element of production archived and coordinated in a powerful database. The *Washington Post* has recently replaced its

(American) SII editorial system with CCI Newsdesk, proof that European companies can still compete in the global market. Newsdesk integrates Word into its editorial function but has its own page layout system (LayoutChamp) which the company describes as being 'in line with contemporary state-of-the-art desktop products'. That suggests a similarity to QuarkXPress.

Quark has for some years been the industry standard when it comes to professional DTP software and its story is yet another demonstration of the benefits of following the trailblazer. In 1987 a serious and well-researched book called simply *Desktop Publishing* (Kirty Wilson-Davies *et al.*) noted that Adobe's Pagemaker program had 'set standards and become regarded as the benchmark that other software developers must follow if they are to win a slice of the market'. Quark is not even mentioned here, nor in Graham Jones's *The Desktop Publishing Companion* (1987), which also commends Pagemaker.

Three years later the BBC book *Into Print: How To Make Desktop Publishing Work For You* could state, 'XPress is the designer's or typographer's layout program. It represents the state of the art in page makeup.' Quark did everything which Pagemaker did and then added tremendous control over typography, a more flexible approach to layout and better handling of graphics.

QuarkXPress was originally only available for the Macintosh, but over the years it has added features and functions and become available for the PC as well. The development of QPS as a complete publishing environment has helped to keep it at the top of the tree. As you would expect from such a powerful program, it takes some time to learn to use it all, although the basic functions can be picked up quickly.

Pagemaker has also changed over the years, and although it is a very popular product it has never quite penetrated the professional market as effectively as XPress. Adobe seems to have acknowledged this by introducing a newer package called InDesign which can be used in conjunction with InCopy, a specialised word processor for writers and subeditors.

When InDesign was introduced it was hailed in many quarters as a potential 'Quark killer'. It took the best features of Pagemaker (and XPress) and added better incorporation of graphics and web access. The plan didn't quite come off, but many of the large system integrators now offer InDesign either in place of, or as an alternative to, XPress.

This kind of incorporation, or convergence, is taken to a higher level in what is, at the time of writing, the latest development in newsroom systems – the prototype Newsplex newsroom being built at the University of South Carolina. Newsplex is intended to come to terms with a future in which:

the successful newspaper will not be confined to the Worldwide Web but will encompass e-mail, pagers, PDA and cell phone services, radio and Internet radio, TV, streaming TV, database information services, Inter-active TV services, peer-to-peer networks, and services to specialized devices, such as MP3 players.

(Ifra Trend Report 109)

That's quite a wish list but it is endorsed by Ifra, the world's leading associa-tion for media publishing and one of the driving forces behind Newsplex; other participants include publishing groups and systems suppliers from the US, Switzerland, Denmark and the UK's own Guardian Media Group.

Newsplex is described as 'a beyond-the-state-of-the-art facility for training, development, demonstration and research in next-generation, cross-media news handling methodologies and technologies'. It is the combination of those two '-ologies' which is important and interesting. Far from being just a testbed for new kit, Newsplex will operate as a real newsroom of the future and concentrate on studying the way news flows and how journalists can work most effectively in a multimedia environment.

Ifra's director of technology, Kerry J. Northrup, explains: 'I would visit news-papers to discuss future visions of the industry and it would get to a point where the newspapers would say "This all sounds very good, but where can we see this future vision in practice", and I had to say that it did not exist. Now I can point to Newsplex.'

South Carolina's $1.5m facility will come into operation in 2002, but even if it proves to be a flawed vision, we can make a definite statement about the future of publishing equipment. The one universal characteristic of new tech-nology is that it is always new. There is little point in trying to describe to you how to operate different systems or even to suggest which system is best. By next year (whichever year you're reading this) something might have come along to make QuarkXPress look as quaint as the Linotypes in Brecon museum's film. It is a fact of life that as a subeditor you will probably have to adapt to using several different technologies during a working lifetime. Get used to the idea now.

Weblog

www.ifra.com   www.newsops.com
www.cci.dk   www.net-linx.com
www.adobe.com   www.quark.com
www.colegroup.com   www.seyboldreport.com

Tim Holmes

13
Website subbing

In the digital world the role of subediting is vital. Mark Day of the *Australian* newspaper says that 'vastly expanded communications facilities through the internet bring the work of teams of reporters into newsrooms a world away where subeditors, rather than correspondents, pluck out the various elements which make up a story' (www.theaustralian.news.com.au/printpage/0,5942,2421975,00.html).

And Renee Moody of *Independent Online*, part of Independent News and Media in South Africa says:

> It's hard work but it's fun. You have a structure based on the sub's role – selecting the copy, and processing the pictures. Plus there's a duty editor . . . who's sitting there juggling the potential stories for the front page as well as watching the wires for agency stories. It's multitasking at its peak.
>
> (via www.ifra.com)

Anyone who works on a website is likely to have a portfolio of tasks, one of which will be subediting. As Helen Nicholson at BBC Online Newcastle says: 'When a journalist writes a story they're not just responsible for the words: they're also responsible for the subbing, the pictures and the overall design of the page.'

She stresses the portfolio aspect: 'In my experience there is no such thing as a "web subeditor" in the BBC, so anyone applying for a job as a broadcast assistant or a broadcast journalist has to be a jack-of-all-trades.'

This point is emphasised by Graham Jenkins of Scrum.com, Sportal's rugby site, whose advice is to 'be multi-skilled, because unless there is a large editorial budget behind the company, a team of subs who do only that is a real luxury'.

But the 'digital world' extends beyond the website: before too long there will be mobile devices which combine the roles of phones, personal digital assistants (PDAs) and computers, and people will access journalistic output on them. Mobile phone and PDA users already have the opportunity to do this, although the limitations of WAP technology circumscribe what can be accessed. Processing content into the different formats, often done automatically, can also create problems when judged by traditional subbing standards.

And that's what we're talking about here – the limitations of the technology, of the screen, of the time which people will devote to looking for and reading this material. One aspect of the subeditor's role has always been to allow readers to make the most of their time: tightening sloppy copy means more stories per issue; correcting errors means more trust and commitment; putting things in order of importance allows a hurried scan to reveal the main points of the main stories. In the digital world of computer, PDA and phone screens the subeditor has to be aware of what works most effectively and tailor the material accordingly. As the technology and applications develop, so the digital journalist must keep pace; this truly is lifelong learning.

Just as not all reading devices are equal, neither are all locations. There are millions of digital sites online, but as far as subediting goes they can be divided into two major types, informative and entertaining. There is a third type, where subediting is largely irrelevant, which can be characterised as un-mediated. An example is www.slashdot.org, a site that specialises in allowing people to communicate with each other. This and similar sites became very busy after the attack on the World Trade Center and many journalists turned to them to find information (often eyewitness accounts) and to judge the general mood.

Whether these sites are absolutely unmediated is a moot point. The laws of defamation still apply in cyberspace, even though they are applied differently in different countries (see below).

Informative sites

Ask yourself two questions – why are people visiting this site and where are they from?

The answer to the first is they want information and they want it immediately. They do not want to be enticed into reading something.

As for the second, they could be from anywhere in the world and this brings with it potential problems with language skills and specific cultural references.

Thus, if you think of subbing for a digital news site as being like subbing for a tabloid newspaper, only simpler, you will be in the right area.

Headlines must be clear. Helen Nicholson says that '[print] magazines can get away with clever, often obscure, headlines, but on the web it's preferable for the headline to be explanatory and leave the user in no doubt as to what story it refers to'. The same stricture applies to the punning headlines beloved of tabloids. Length is also important; the BBC style guide for online journalists states: 'If a headline is longer than six words, stop and think again.'

Although the speed of operation precludes many dummy pages being created, the warning about obscene language applies here as much as in print. However, the headline 'Fucks off to Benfica' which appeared on Eurosport.com in June 2001 was an example not of such a mistake, but of a deliberate 'joke' – the story concerned footballer Angelico Fucks who had transferred from FC Porto to Benfica. Although similar wordplay has appeared in newspapers and magazines over the years, the question of its acceptability should always be considered. Perhaps a sport site on the internet has sufficient licence to be adolescent (www.eurosport.com/News.asp?StoryID=102878&SportID=22& FetchDate=2001–06–06&LangueID=0).

Below the headline, stories on digital sites must be very tightly written, using plain, unambiguous language.

News stories should follow the inverted pyramid format whatever the medium, but it is more applicable than ever here – especially if copy is destined for mobile phones and PDAs. The BBC guide recommends that reporters pack as much information as possible into the first four paragraphs, including essential background or context. Important stories get 400–500 words, lesser ones 250–350.

Deeper background can be included after the fourth par, but even then online journalists should remember that it is just as easy to add a link to archived or extra material and allow readers to look it up or not as they choose. These extras can include audio and video clips, which the journalist is also responsible for loading.

Even though clear headlines and condensed copy help readers to read, the story still needs to be projected on the page. The audio-visual extras may attract but traditional subediting elements like subheads, pull quotes and sidebars (or fact boxes) help to bring the screen to life.

Bulleted lists are also a good technique for summarising a complicated story, and they can sometimes prove essential just to keep a site online. When CNN.com started to overload on 11 September 2001 as millions of people tried to access it, this major site stripped its output down to a single screen of bulleted headlines-cum-summaries to keep people informed, while engineers added more server power.

Entertainment sites

The situation is slightly different here. No one turns to a site like www. peoplenews.com* because they want to be kept abreast of current affairs; the very fact that you have logged on to it demonstrates that you have time to waste, so a different set of rules applies.

Nevertheless, remember that reading on screen is still not as pleasant or easy as reading off paper; very few people actively want to scroll down reams of text. Paul Newman, editor of *Internet Made Easy*, says: 'Web subbing requires the use of much smaller paragraphs, particularly for features, and you should be careful which symbols you use as not all will display in a web browser.' (Technical considerations are considered below.) Joe Goodden of BBC Online in Wales adds: 'It's not uncommon to see an article consisting solely of one-sentence paragraphs.'

Joe raises another interesting point in relation to the interactivity with readers which online publishing not only allows but positively encourages:

> In the BBC we try to include a lot of user-generated content, because we're publicly funded and have to represent the people. A large amount is taken from users' emails and message boards. It's important that we don't change people's words, so spelling mistakes tend to get left in. Of course this depends on the end purpose and the context of publication. For example a teen website like *www.bbc.co.uk/so/weird* might have letters published which are predominantly written in txt msg style. However, this wouldn't be the case on the Talking Points section of *news.bbc.co.uk*, where copy is much more likely to be tidied up.

Subediting thus becomes a relative term. All copy has to be checked for libel or obscenity but acceptable styles may vary enormously even within the same site.

A third universal requirement is accuracy under pressure – and the pressure is even greater than on a newspaper because as soon as a story has been written it goes straight out. Even here, however, there is a twist. Helen Nicholson puts it well:

> You check everything thoroughly before it goes live but I'm sure many mistakes are overlooked because it hasn't been checked by a sub. The key difference is that a magazine cannot be republished once it has hit the newsagent's shelves, but an online publication can correct the mistake in minutes and republish the page. But of course it's impera- tive that BBC sites don't contain errors.

* This site was extant, just, at the time of writing. If it has since disappeared into the wastes of cyberspace, try www.hello-magazine.co.uk. If all else fails take a look at www.tarapt.com.

And not just BBC ones, either. Graham Jenkins recalled this embarrassing episode from Scrum.com:

> One of our team questioned England manager Clive Woodward's knowledge of his own team, suggesting he didn't know the identity of one young player who had toured North America in the summer. This was pointed out to him and in an email to the entire rugby journalist fraternity he labelled us 'totalbollocks.com', said he had never heard of our site and would be giving it a wide berth in future. By the time we pulled the piece every rugby journalist had seen it and it appeared in the papers the next day.

Sites which publish in multiple formats may encounter a more complicated version of this problem. Patrick O'Brien, editor of *Mergers & Acquisitions Impact* – a purely digital publication – recalls an incident when a large American computer company complained about a factual error in a piece he had written:

> Although the story had already been sent out in an email attachment to all subscribers, they were placated by the fact that I'd changed the web-based version immediately. Not that such flexibility should lead to sloppiness, of course.

Legal issues

The internet is still developing as a publishing medium and legal problems are developing with it. The laws of defamation have not changed but they are being interpreted differently in different countries and, given the net's global reach, this is an area which requires constant monitoring.

In the UK, a website and the service provider (ISP) which hosts it are held responsible if they allow defamatory material to be posted, no matter where such material originated. A landmark case brought against Demon Internet, one of the largest ISPs in the UK, established this precedent in 1999; see www.cyber-rights.org/reports/demon.htm for a full analysis.

In the US, on the other hand, Section 230 of the Communications Decency Act states that 'No provider or user of an interactive computer service shall be treated as the publisher or speaker of any information provided by another information content provider,' This has been used to shield companies such as AOL from liability for illegal statements written by subscribers.

However, on 25 July 2001, Judge James A. Richman of the California superior court ruled that the same section applied to individuals as well as ISPs, and that an individual's repeated repostings to news groups of an allegedly libellous message originally written and posted by another person was protected by federal law. Commentators concluded it was the judge's opinion that anyone who reposted defamatory material was shielded from liability, although the original author of a libel posted on the internet might be subject to legal action and damages. This case is discussed at www.nytimes.com/2001/08/09/technology/10CYBERLAW.html, but as the defendants intended to appeal this is unlikely to be the final word.

Meanwhile, in a landmark case in Australia, Victoria Supreme Court has ruled that a businessman can take American financial publisher Dow Jones to court in Melbourne, his home city. Although Dow Jones argued that the allegedly defamatory material originated in New York, the court found that the nature of the internet meant the article had also been published in Australia and could be tried there. (Reported in *Australian IT*, 29 August 2001 and posted in the IFRA newsletter.)

Given the speed and extent of developments it is essential for all online journalists to keep an eye on the media and legal pages in newspapers, trade press and websites for updates in this area.

Technical issues

The word technical, in this context, has two meanings – traditional elements of the craft of subediting and the technological demands made of a digital subeditor.

Craft

On the one hand, Helen Nicholson of BBC Online in Newcastle can say about this form of publishing: 'You don't have to worry about the dreaded widows and orphans.' But on the other, Patrick O'Brien is concerned with precisely this problem, created by the various forms of *Mergers & Acquisitions Impact*:

> As we publish on the web and in email attachments simultaneously, it is almost impossible to sort out widows and orphans as the text goes through an automated process for each of the different formats. Time constraints and resources mean that going into each format again to sort this out manually is impractical. The result? Widows and orphans everywhere.

This is a young medium and there are, as yet, very few rules which have been set in stone. But that is no reason why old craft skills should be abandoned if they are still useful. On a small screen, a widow represents a large proportion of the reading area, and this should certainly be taken into consideration.

Similarly, making copy easy to read does not just mean cutting it to the bone, it can also mean the physical legibility of words on screen – the province of the sub's ancient friend, typography.

Eddie Bissell, a journalism educator who runs Training Direct International and lectures at Derby University, puts this at the top of his list for effective website subbing, along with an understanding of hyphenation and screen size. 'For me,' he says, 'writing and subbing for websites involve reducing the need to make the reader scroll, an appreciation of founts and sizes for good readability, and co-ordinating the colours of type and background.'

Type which works well in print may not look as good or be as easy to read in the pixellated environment of the computer screen (let alone on a mobile phone). New founts intended for digital publishing have been drawn up and there are doubtless many more to come. Trade titles and magazines or websites aimed at designers will carry news of developments, examples of their use and hints and tips for effective execution. The original, and still one of the best, site for dissemination of information and opinion about the usability of websites is Dr Jakob Nielsen's useit.com; anyone connected with this line of work should consult it regularly.

Remember also that earlier warning about the use of certain symbols. In an article about proofreading online, American editor Kathy Henning recommends writers to read their pages on different platforms and in different browsers:

> Check the text on a Mac and PC, in Internet Explorer and Netscape. If your audience comprises a substantial percentage of AOL users . . . check the text in AOL, too . . . Proof any text in all caps separately and more painstakingly. Typos and misspellings are much more difficult to see in all caps . . . Proof the most prominent text separately. Ironically, the most prominent text is often the most easily overlooked.
>
> (www.clickz.com/article/cz.3494.html)

Technology

Aspects of this have already been covered in passing, such as the need for a digital journalist to be skilled in the use of still and moving words (copy and audio), and still and moving pictures (photographs and video). There are many different software packages in use but among the most prominent are Cool Edit Pro and Real for audio, PhotoShop for stills, Premiere and Real for video, Dreamweaver for website creation and Flash for animation.

The HTML code which underlies most web-based creations should also be familiar to a competent digital journalist, along with protocols like TCP/IP which permit remote communication. Then there are proprietary creations like the BBC's database-driven Content Production System (CPS) to get to grips with (though that example is straightforward enough).

Such variety can make a job varied, interesting and challenging. As one BBC Online journalist says: 'It's a dynamic industry that allows people to take part in all kinds of tasks down the publishing line, rather than just sticking to subbing.'

But there is another side to it. Jon Wright has worked on websites for News International, among others, and he has also been a staff writer and freelance for numerous print magazines. He does not recall the newspaper sites with any great fondness: 'My memories of the *Sun* and *News of the World* are that the work was mechanised and dull.' He has these words of advice for anyone thinking of taking up employment online:

> Be careful before accepting a web job if your dream is, say, to launch a magazine. Web work can take you away from print work and the technical skills needed are different.

Weblog

www.useit.com
www.ifra.com

Tim Holmes

Glossary of terms used in journalism

Journalism is rich in jargon. Some of it comes from printing (book for magazine); or survives from the pre-computer age (spike for rejected copy); or is imported from the United States (clippings for cuttings). It is often punchy and graphic (ambush, bust, fireman). But if it crops up in copy (eg in stories about the media) the sub will usually have to change it (replace 'story' by 'report') or explain it (after 'chapel' insert 'office branch' in brackets). The obvious exception is in publications for journalists such as *Press Gazette* and the *Journalist*.

ABC: Audit Bureau of Circulation – source of independently verified circulation figures
ad: advertisement
add: extra copy to add to existing story
advance: 1 text of speech or statement issued to journalists beforehand; 2 expenses paid before a trip
advertorial: advertisement presented as editorial
agencies: news agencies, eg PA and Reuters
agony column: regular advice given on personal problems sent in by readers; hence agony aunt
ambush: journalists lying in wait for unsuspecting, unwilling interviewee
ampersand: & – symbol for 'and'
angle: particular approach to story, journalist's point of view in writing it
art editor: visual journalist responsible for design and layout of publication
artwork: illustrations (eg drawings, photographs) prepared for reproduction
ascender: the part of a lower-case letter (eg b and d) that sticks out above the x-height in a typeface
attribution: identifying the journalist's source of information or quote
author's (corrections, marks): proof corrections by writer of story

back number, issue: previous issue of publication
back of the book: second part of magazine (after the centre spread)
backbench, the: senior newspaper journalists who make key production decisions
backgrounder: explanatory feature to accompany news story
bad break: clumsy hyphenation at the end of a line
banner (headline): one in large type across front page

basket: where copy goes – once a physical basket, now a digital folder
bastard measure: type set to a width that is not standard for the page
beard: the space between a letter and the edge of the base on which it is designed
beat: American term for specialist area covered by reporter
bill(board): poster promoting edition of newspaper, usually highlighting main news story
black: duplicate of written story (from colour of carbon paper once used with typewriter)
bleed: (of an image) go beyond the type area to the edge of a page
blob: solid black circle used for display effect or to tabulate lists
blob par: extra paragraph introduced by blob
blow up: enlarge (part of) photograph
blown quote: another term for pull quote
blurb: displayed material promoting contents of another page or future issue
body copy: the main text of a story, as opposed to page furniture
body type: the main typeface in which a story is set (as opposed to display)
bold: thick black type, used for emphasis
book: printer's (and so production journalist's) term for magazine
bot: black on tone
box: copy enclosed by rules to give it emphasis and/or separate it from the main text
breaker: typographical device, eg crosshead, used to break up text on the page
brief: 1 short news item; 2 instruction to journalist on how to approach story
bring up: bring forward part of story to earlier position
broadsheet: large-format newspaper such as the *Guardian*
bromide: photographic print
bullet (point): another term for blob
bureau: office of news agency or newspaper office in foreign country
business-to-business: current term for what were once called 'trade' magazines, ie those covering a business area, profession, craft or trade
bust: (of a headline) be too long for the space available
buy-up interview: exclusive bought by publication
byline: writer's name as it appears in print at the beginning of a story

c & lc: capital and lower-case letters
call out: another term for pull quote
calls (also check calls): routine phone calls made by reporters to organisations such as police and fire brigade to see if a story is breaking
camera-ready: (eg artwork) prepared for reproduction
caps: capital letters
caption: words used with a picture (usually underneath), identifying where necessary and relating it to the accompanying story
caption story: extension of picture caption into a self-contained story
cast off: estimate amount of printed matter copy would make
casual: journalist employed by the shift
catch(line): short word (not printed) identifying different elements of a story in the editorial process
centre: set type with equal space on either side

centre spread: middle opening of tabloid or magazine

chapel: office branch of media union (the shop steward is the father, FoC, or mother, MoC, of the chapel)

character: unit of measurement for type including letters, figures, punctuation marks and spaces

chequebook journalism: paying large sums for stories

chief sub: senior subeditor in charge of the others

city desk: financial section of British national newspaper (in the US the city desk covers home news)

classified advertising: small ads 'classified' by subject matter, grouped in a separate section

clippings/clips: American term for cuttings

close quotes: end of section in direct quotes

close up: reduce space between lines, words or characters

CMYK: cyan, magenta, yellow and black, the process (basic printing) colours

col: column

colour piece: news story written as feature with emphasis on journalist's reactions

colour sep(aration)s: method by which the four process colours (CMYK) are separated from a colour original

column: 1 standard vertical division of page; 2 regular feature by journalist often encouraged to be opinionated and/or entertaining

column rule: light rule between columns of type

conference: meeting of editorial staff to plan current/next issue

consumer magazines: the category includes specialist titles (eg *Angling Times*), women's magazines and those of general interest

contact sheet: photographer's sheet of small prints

contacts book: a journalist's list of contacts with details of phone, fax, email etc

contents bill: *see* bill

controlled circulation: free distribution of specialist title to target readership by geography (free newspapers) or interest group (business-to-business magazines)

copy: text of story

copy taster: *see* taster

copyright: right to reproduce original material

copytaker: telephone typist who takes down copy from reporter

corr: correspondent

correction: published statement correcting errors in story

correspondent: journalist covering specialist area, eg education

coverlines: selling copy on front cover

credit (line): name of photographer or illustrator as it appears in print next to their work

Cromalins: the Dupont system of glossy colour proofs

crop: cut (image) to size or for better effect

crosshead: line or lines, taken from the text, set bigger and bolder than the body type and inserted between paragraphs to liven up page

cut: shorten or delete copy

cut-out: illustration with background masked, painted or cut to make it stand out on the page

cuts: cuttings

cuttings: stories taken (originally cut) from newspapers and filed electronically under subject

cuttings job: story that is over-dependent on cuttings

dateline: place from which copy is filed

deadline: time story (or any part of it) is due

deck: originally one of a series of headlines stacked on top of each other; now usually used to mean one line of a headline

delayed drop: device in news story of delaying important facts for effect

delete: remove

descender: the part of a lower-case letter (eg g and j) that sticks out below the x-height in a typeface

desk: newspaper department, eg picture desk

deskman: American term for male subeditor

diary, the: list of news events to be covered; hence an off-diary story is one originated by the reporter

diary column: gossip column

direct input: transmission of copy direct from the journalist's keyboard to the computer for typesetting (as opposed to the old system in which compositors retyped copy)

disclaimer: statement explaining that a particular person or organisation was not the subject of a previously published story

display ads: ordinary (not 'classified') ads which appear throughout a publication

display type: type for headlines etc

district reporter: one covering a particular area away from the main office

doorstepping: reporters lying in wait for (usually) celebrities outside their homes

double: a story published twice in the same issue of a publication

double-column: (of text, headline, illustration) across two columns

double (page) spread: two facing pages in a magazine, whether advertising or editorial

downtable subs: those other than the chief sub and deputies

drop cap, letter: outsize initial capital letter used to start story or section; it drops down alongside the text which is indented to accommodate it

drop quotes: outsize quotes used to mark quoted matter

dummy: 1 pre-publication edition of new publication used to sell advertising and experiment editorially; 2 blank version of publication, eg to show quality and weight of paper; 3 complete set of page proofs

edition: version of newspaper printed for particular circulation area or time

editor: senior journalist responsible for publication or section

editorial: 1 leading article expressing editorial opinion; 2 content that is not advertising

editor's conference: main planning meeting for next issue

em, en: units of measurement for type – the width of the two letters m and n

embargo: time before which an organisation supplying material, eg by press release, does not want it published

ends: the story ends here

EPD: electronic picture desk

EPS file: Encapsulated PostScript file
exclusive: claim by publication that it has a big story nobody else has
exes: journalists' out-of-pocket expenses

face: type design
facing matter: (of advertising) opposite editorial
facsimile: exact reproduction, as with electronic transmission of pages
feature: article that goes beyond reporting of facts to explain and/or entertain;
    also used of any editorial material that is not news or listings; hence feature
    writer, features editor
file: transmit copy
filler: short news item to fill space
fireman: traditional term for reporter sent to trouble spot when story breaks
fit: (of copy etc) to occupy exactly the space available
flannel panel: magazine's address, contact information and list of staff
flash: brief urgent message from news agency
flatplan: page-by-page plan of issue
flip: (of picture) transpose left to right
flush left or right: (of type) having one consistent margin with the other ragged
fold, the: centre fold in a newspaper so that only the upper half of the paper
    ('above the fold') is visible at the point of sale
folio: page (number)
follow up: take published story as the starting point for an update
format: 1 size, shape or style of publication or section; 2 computer instruction;
    hence to format
fount (pronounced font and now often spelt that way): typeface
free(sheet): free newspaper
freebie: something useful or pleasant, often a trip, supplied free to journalists
freelance: self-employed journalist who sells material to various outlets
freelancer: American term for freelance
fudge: another term for stop press
full out: (of type) not indented

galley proof: typeset proof not yet made up into a page
gatefold: an extra page which folds out from a magazine
ghost writer: journalist writing on behalf of someone else, often by interviewing
    them; hence to ghost (eg a column)
gone to bed: passed for press so too late for corrections
grams per square metre (gsm; g/m²): the measure used to define the weight of
    paper
graphics: visual material, usually drawn
grid: design skeleton specifying (eg) number and width of columns
gutter: space between two facing pages; can also be used of space between
    columns

H & J: (of copy on screen) hyphenated and justified, so in the form in which it
    will be typeset
hack, hackette: jocular terms for journalist
hair space: thinnest space between typeset letters

half-tone: illustration broken into dots of varying sizes
handout: printed material, eg press release, distributed to journalists
hanging indent: copy set with first line of each paragraph full out and subsequent ones indented
hard copy: copy on paper, eg printout, rather than screen
head, heading: headline
heavy: broadsheet newspaper
heavy type: thicker than standard
hold (over): keep material for future use
hot metal: old typesetting system in which type was cast from molten metal
house ad: publisher's advertisement in its own publication
house journal: publication for employees of a particular organisation
house style: the way a publication chooses to publish in matters of detail

imposition: arrangement of pages for printing
imprint: name and address of publisher and printer
in-house: inside a media organisation
in pro: in proportion (used of visual material to be reduced)
indent: set copy several characters in from left-hand margin
input: type copy into computer
insert: 1 extra copy to be included in existing story; 2 printed matter inserted in publication after printing and binding
intro: first paragraph of story; also used (confusingly) in some magazine offices to mean standfirst
ISDN: integrated services digital network – a means of transmitting editorial material between offices, to printers etc
italics: italic (sloping) type

jack-line: another word for widow
journo: jocular term for journalist
justified: type set with consistent margins

kern: reduce the space between characters in typeset copy
kicker: introductory part of caption or headline
kill: drop a story; hence kill fee for freelance whose commissioned story is not used
knocking copy: story written with negative angle

label: (of headline) without a verb
landscape: horizontal picture
layout: arrangement of body type, headlines etc and illustrations on the page
lead: 1 main story on a page; 2 tip-off or idea for story (in the US the intro of a story is called the lead)
leader: leading article expressing editorial opinion
leader dots: three dots used to punctuate
leading (pronounced 'ledding'): space between lines (originally made by inserting blank slugs of lead between lines of type)
leg: column of typeset copy
legal: send material to be checked for legal problems, eg libel

legal kill: lawyer's instruction not to use
lensman: American term for male photographer
letter spacing: space between letters
libel: defamatory statement in permanent or broadcast form
lift: 1 use all or most of a story taken from one newspaper edition in the next; 2 steal a story from another media outlet and reproduce it with few changes
ligature: two or more joined letters
light face: type lighter than standard
linage (this spelling preferred to lineage): payment to freelances by the line; also refers to classified advertising without illustration
line drawing: drawing made up of black strokes
listings: lists of entertainment and other events with basic details
literal: typographical error
lobby, the: specialist group of political reporters covering parliament
local corr: local correspondent
logo: name, title or recognition word in particular design used on regular section or column; also used of magazine's front-page title
lower case: ordinary letters (not caps)

make-up: assembly of type and illustrations on the page ready for reproduction
mark up: specify the typeface, size and width in which copy is to be set
masking: covering part of photograph for reproduction
masthead: publication's front-page title
measure: width of typesetting
medium type: between light and heavy
merchandising: details of stockists and prices in consumer features
mf: more copy follows
model release: contract signed by photographic model authorising use of pictures
mono(chrome): printed in one colour, usually black
more: more copy follows
mug shot: photograph showing head (and sometimes shoulders)
must: copy that must appear, eg apology or correction
mutton: old name for an em

neg: photographic negative
news agency: supplier of news and features to media outlets
news desk: organising centre of newsroom
newsman: American term for male reporter
newsprint: standard paper on which newspapers are printed
newsroom: news reporters' room
nib: news in brief – short news item
night lawyer: barrister who reads newspaper proofs for legal problems
nose: intro of story; hence to renose – rewrite intro
NUJ: National Union of Journalists
nut: old name for an en; hence nutted, type indented one en

obit: obituary
off-diary: *see* diary, the

off-the-record: statements made to a journalist on the understanding that they will not be reported directly or attributed

on spec: uncommissioned (material submitted by freelance)

on-the-record: statements made to a journalist that can be reported and attributed

op-ed: feature page facing page with leading articles

open quotes: start of section in direct quotes

originals: photographs or other visual material for reproduction

orphan: first line of a paragraph at the foot of a page or column

out take: another term for pull quote

overlay: sheet of transparent paper laid over artwork with instructions on how to process it

overline: another word for strapline

overmatter: typset material that does not fit the layout and must be cut

overprint: print over a previously printed background

PA: Press Association, Britain's national news agency

package: main feature plus sidebars

page furniture: displayed type, eg headlines, standfirsts and captions, used to project copy

page plan: editorial instructions for layout

page proof: proof of a made-up page

pagination: the number of pages in a publication; also a newspaper system's ability to make up pages

panel: another word for box

par, para: paragraph

paparazzo/i: photographer(s) specialising in pursuing celebrities

paste-up: page layout pasted into position

patch: specialist area covered by reporter

pay-off: final twist or flourish in the last paragraph of a story

peg: reason for publishing feature at a particular time

photomontage: illustration created by combining several photographs

pic, pix: press photograph(s)

pica: unit of type measurement

pick-up (of photographs): those that already exist and can therefore be picked up by journalists covering a story

picture desk: organising centre of collection and editing of pictures

piece: article

plate: printing image carrier from which pages are printed

point: 1 full stop; 2 standard unit of type size

pool: group of reporters sharing information and releasing it to other media organisations

PostScript: Adobe's page description language

PR(O): public relations (officer); hence someone performing a public relations role

press cuttings: see cuttings

press release: written announcement or promotional material by organisation sent to media outlets and individual journalists

profile: portrait in words of individual or organisation

proof: printout of part or whole of page so it can be checked and corrected

proofread: check proofs; hence proofreader

publisher: 1 publishing company; 2 individual in magazine publishing company with overall responsibility for title or group of titles
puff: story promoting person or organisation
pull: proof; to pull is to take a proof
pull (out) quote (blown quote, call out, out take): short extract from text set in larger type as part of page layout
pullout: separate section of publication that can be pulled out
pyramid: (usually inverted) conventional structure for news story with most important facts in intro

query: question mark
queue: collection of stories held in a computer
quote: verbatim quotation
quotes: quotation marks

ragged: (of type) with uneven margin
raised cap: outsize initial capital letter used to start story or section; it is raised above the text
range left or right: (of type) have one consistent margin with the other ragged
register: alignment of coloured inks on the printed page
rejig: rewrite copy, particularly in the light of later information
renose: rewrite intro of a story
reporter: gatherer and writer of news
repro house: company that processes colour pictures ready for printing
retainer: regular payment to local correspondent or freelance
retouch: alter photograph to emphasise particular feature
Reuters: international news agency
reverse indent: another term for hanging indent
reversed out: (type) printed in white on black or tinted background
revise: extra proof to check that corrections have been made
rewrite: write new version of story or section as opposed to subbing on copy
ring-round: story based on series of phone calls
river: white space running down a column of type, caused by space between words
roman: plain upright type
rough: sketch for layout
round-up: gathering of disparate elements for single story
RSI: repetitive strain injury, attributed to overuse and misuse of computer keyboard, mouse etc
rule: line between columns or round illustrations
run: period of printing an edition or number of copies printed
run on: (of type) continue from one line, column or page to the next
running foot: title and issue date at the foot of the page
running head: title and issue date at the top of the page
running story: one that is constantly developing, over a newspaper's different editions or a number of days
running turns: pages with no paragraph breaks on first and last lines; also used of columns
rush: second most urgent message from news agency (after flash)

sans (serif): plain type (*see* serif) – this is an example
scaling (of pictures): calculating depth
schedule: 1 list of jobs for (eg) reporters; 2 publication's printing programme
scheme: make a plan of page layout
scoop: jocular word for exclusive
screamer: exclamation mark
screen: the number of dots per square inch of a half-tone
section: 1 separately folded part of newspaper; 2 complete printed sheet making up part of magazine
sell: another word for standfirst, often used in women's magazines
serif: decorative addition to type – this is an example
set and hold: typeset and keep for use later
setting: copy set in type
shift: daily stint worked by staff journalists and casuals
shoot: a photographic session
shy: (of headline) too short for the space available
sidebar: subsidiary story or other material placed next to main story, usually in box
sidehead: subsidiary heading, set flush left
sign-off: writer's name as it appears in print at the end of a story
sketch: light-hearted account of events, especially parliamentary
slip: newspaper edition for particular area or event
small caps: capital letters in smaller size of the same typeface
snap: early summary by news agency of important story to come
snapper: jocular term for press photographer
snaps: press photographs
solid: (of type) set without extra leading
spike: where rejected copy goes (originally a metal spike)
splash: newspaper's main front-page story
splash sub: subeditor responsible for tabloid's front page
spoiler: attempt by newspaper to reduce impact of rival's exclusive by publishing similar story
spot colour: second colour (after black) used in printing publication
spread: two facing pages
s/s: same size
standfirst: introductory matter accompanying headline, particularly used in features
stet: ignore deletion or correction (Latin for 'let it stand')
stone: bench where pages were made up; hence stone sub – subeditor who makes final corrections and cuts on page proofs
stop press: small area on back page of newspaper left blank for late news in days of hot metal
story: article, especially news report
strap(line): subsidiary headline above main headline
Street, the: Fleet Street, where many newspapers once had their offices
stringer: local correspondent; freelance on contract to a news organisation
style: house style
stylebook/style sheet: where house style is recorded
sub: subeditor

subhead: subsidiary headline
subtitle: another word for standfirst

tabloid: popular small-format newspaper such as the *Sun*
tagline: explanatory note under headline
take: section of copy for setting
take back: (on proof) take words back to previous line
take over: (on proof) take words forward to next line
taster: production journalist who checks and selects copy; also coverline
think piece: feature written to show and provoke thought
tie-in: story connected with the one next to it
tint: shaded area on which type can be printed
tip(-off): information supplied (and usually paid for) whether by freelance or member of the public
titlepiece: traditional term for name of magazine as it appears on the cover – now replaced by masthead and logo
TOT: triumph over tragedy, feature formula particularly popular in women's magazines
tracking: space between characters
trade names: product names (eg Hoover, Kleenex, Velcro)
tranny: transparency – photograph in film form
trans(pose): reverse order
turn: part of story continued on a later page
typeface: a complete range of type in a particular style, eg Times New Roman
typescale: measuring rule for type
typo: American term for typographical error
typography: craft of using type

u/lc: upper and lower case
underscore: underline
unj(ustified): text set flush left, ragged right
upper and lower case: mixture of capitals and ordinary letters
upper case: capital letters

vignette: illustration whose edges gradually fade to nothing
vox pop: series of street interviews (Latin: *vox populi* – voice of the people)

weight: thickness or boldness of letters in a typeface
white space: area on page with no type or illustration
widow: single word or part of word at the end of a paragraph on a line by itself; originally the last line of a paragraph at the top of a page or column
wire: a means of transmitting copy by electronic signal; hence wire room
wob: white on black – type reversed out
wot: white on tone

x-height: height of the lower-case letters of a typeface (excluding ascenders and descenders)

Further reading

English usage and writing style

Blamires, Harry, *Correcting your English*, Bloomsbury, 1996

Bryson, Bill, *Troublesome Words*, Viking, 2001

Burchfield, R. W. (ed.), *The New Fowler's Modern English Usage*, 3rd edn, OUP, 1996

Hicks, Wynford, *English for Journalists*, 2nd edn, Routledge, 1998

—— *Writing for Journalists*, Routledge, 1999

Strunk, William, *The Elements of Style*, 3rd edn, revised by E. B. White, Macmillan (New York), 1979, also available free at www.bartleby.com/141/

Waterhouse, Keith, *Waterhouse on Newspaper Style*, Viking, 1989 (replaces *Daily Mirror Style*, out of print)

Subediting

Evans, Harold, *Essential English for Journalists, Editors and Writers*, revised by Crawford Gillan, Pimlico, 2000 (replaces the Evans Editing and Design series of five books, *Newsman's English*, *Handling Newspaper Text*, *News Headlines*, *Picture Editing*, *Newspaper Design*, all out of print)

Hodgson, F. W., *New Subediting*, 3rd edn, Focal Press, 1998

Sellers, Leslie, *Doing it in Style*, Pergamon, 1968 (out of print)

—— *The Simple Subs Book*, 2nd edn, Pergamon, 1985

House style

Austin, Tim (comp.), *The Times Guide to English Style and Usage*, Times Books, 1999

The Economist Style Guide, Profile Books, 2000

Inman, Colin (comp.), *The Financial Times Style Guide*, Pitman, 1994

Macdowall, Ian (comp.), *Reuters Handbook for Journalists*, Butterworth-Heinemann, 1992

Marsh, David and Marshall, Nikki (eds), *The Guardian Style Guide*, available free at www.guardian.co.uk

Ritter, R. M. (ed. and comp.), *The Oxford Dictionary for Writers and Editors*, 2nd edn, OUP, 2000

Reference

Army List, Ministry of Defence, Stationery Books Office, 2001

Bartholomew's Gazetteer, John Bartholomew, 1998

Brewer's Dictionary of Modern Phrase and Fable, Adrian Room (ed.), Cassell Reference, 2000

Brewer's Dictionary of Phrase and Fable, Adrian Room (ed.), Cassell Reference, 1999

Burke's Peerage, Charles Mosley (ed.), Fitzroy Dearborn, 1999

The Chambers Dictionary, Chambers, 1998

Crockford's Clerical Directory, Church House Publishing, 2001

Dictionary of Quotations, Elizabeth Knowles (ed.), OUP, 1999

The Guinness Book of Records, Guinness World Records Ltd, 2001

The New Shorter Oxford English Dictionary, Lesley Brown (ed.), OUP, 1993

The Oxford Dictionary of Foreign Words and Phrases, Jennifer Speake (ed.), OUP, 2000

The Oxford Dictionary of Modern Quotations, Tony Augarde (ed.), OUP, 1992

The Oxford Spelling Dictionary, Maurice Waite (ed.), OUP, 2000

Who's Who, Europa Publications, 2002

Others

Barnard, Michael, *Magazine & Journal Production*, Pira International, 1990 (out of print)

Cameron, Deborah, *Verbal Hygiene*, Routledge, 1995

McNae's Essential Law for Journalists, 16th edn, revised by Walter Greenwood and Tom Welsh, Butterworths, 2001

Hall, Jim, *Online Journalism*, Pluto Press, 2001

McGuire, Mary, *et al.*, *The Internet Handbook for Writers, Researchers and Journalists*, Guildford Press, 2000

Mason, Peter and Smith, Derrick, *Magazine Law*, Routledge, 1998

Mayes, Ian, *The Guardian Corrections and Clarifications*, Guardian Newspapers, 2000

Morrish, John, *Magazine Editing*, Routledge, 1996

Reddick, Randy and King, Elliot, *The Online Journalist*, Harcourt Brace, 1997

Ritter, Robert, *The Oxford Guide to Style*, OUP, 2002 (replaces *Hart's Rules for Compositors and Readers at the University Press*, out of print)

Steinberg, S. H., *Five Hundred Years of Printing*, British Library, 1996

Recommended periodicals

Journalist

Press Gazette

Private Eye

Media pages of *Guardian*, *Independent*, *Daily Telegraph*, *Times*, *Observer*

Recommended websites

www.colegroup.com (publishing technology newsletter)

www.honk.co.uk/fleetstreet/forum.htm (journalists' discussion group)

www.ifra.com (publishing developments; free newsletter)

www.useit.com (Jakob Nielsen on digital sites)

www.uta.fi/ethicnet/ethicnet.html (international ethics)

Appendix 1
Bulletin style guide

Bulletin 16/24 is a local newsletter published in English and French circulating in the Charente and Dordogne departments of France.

---

a (not an) historian, hotel etc (but **an** heir, honour etc)
- omit a/an from the titles of organisations (but not books etc)

abbreviations: units of measure are abbreviated and set close-up: a 30m drop, 120kph, a 5kg hammer. But distances and sums of money are not: he fell 20 metres; it cost £1 million.
- Most organisations should be written out in full when first mentioned (the World Health Organisation), then abbreviated (the WHO) but note: the BBC, the IRA.
- Some titles are cumbersome so prefer BSE, mad cow disease; the Gaullist party, the RPR.
- Abbreviations do not take a full point.

see also **acronyms**

accents: keep accents on words of French origin to distinguish résumé from resume, pâté from pate etc

Achilles' heel/tendon (keep cap and apostrophe)

acknowledgement (not acknowledgment)

acronyms: some abbreviations are spoken and written as words with initial cap: Nato, Aids

adaptation (not adaption)

addenda is the plural of addendum

adrenalin (not adrenaline)

adviser (not advisor) but **advisory**

affect (to influence) is confused with **effect** (to accomplish)

ageing (not aging)

agendas is the plural of agenda

aggravate: use to mean make worse, not annoy

aircraft/airplane (not aeroplane)

alibi: use to mean being elsewhere, not excuse

all right (not alright)

Americanisms: write in British English (lift not elevator, pavement not sidewalk, envisage not envision) but note that usage is changing: modern British children are raised more often than brought up and usually play with toy trucks rather than lorries

amid (not amidst)

amok (not amuck)

among (not amongst)

ampersand (&): use only in company names

answerphone: *see also* **trade names** p. 166

anticipate: make use of in advance/expect – don't use

apostrophes: words like men, women and children are plural so the apostrophe goes before the s: children's. In names of places and organisations follow their practice unless it is obviously illiterate: so write Siddalls, Sainsbury's but never womens or womens'. Add an extra s after the apostrophe only if it is sounded: St Thomas's but Achilles' heel/tendon

appendixes is the plural of appendix (both in books and in the body)

approx(imately): use **about**

arguably: possibly/probably – don't use

around: use **about**

artist (not artiste)

assure (to give confidence to) is confused with **ensure** (to make happen) and **insure** (to arrange insurance)

bail (court, cricket)/**bail out** (company, water from boat)

bale (straw)/**bale out** (of airplane)

balk (not baulk)

barbecue (not barbeque, bar-b-q)

beaus is the plural of beau (meaning boyfriend)

beg the question: *see* **clichés**

benefited (not benefitted)

biased (not biassed)

block (not bloc)

blond(e): women are blonde(s); men are blond; women and men have blond hair

bogey (one over par at golf)/**bogie** (railway trolley)/**bogy** (goblin)

bored: by/with (not of)

Brit: don't use

bureaus is the plural of bureau (desk) but **bureaux** is the plural of bureau (office)

burnt (not burned)

bused/busing (not bussed/bussing)

Canute (King): *see* **clichés**

canvas (paint)/**canvass** (for votes)

CAPS/lower case: always prefer lower case – second world war, prime minister

capsize is an exception to the -ise rule

caviar (not caviare)

celibate: unmarried/abstaining from sex – don't use (except in vow of celibacy)

censor (prevent publication) is confused with **censure** (criticise)

centre: in/on (not around/round)

château(x): include circumflex

chauvinist: absurdly nationalistic/sexist – use with care

chronic: use to mean recurrent, not 'very bad'

clichés: try to avoid using them. Never use the ones that people generally get wrong, eg beg the question, the curate's egg, Frankenstein, Hobson's choice and King Canute

cohort: group of people/individual colleague – don't use

collective nouns take either singular or plural verbs (the team is/are) but don't change suddenly from one to the other

combat (verb)/**combated/ing** (not combatted/ing) – but use only in quotes: otherwise use fight/fought/fighting

commence: use **begin** or **start**

compare to (for something completely different – Shall I compare thee to a summer's day?) is confused with **compare with** (like with like – last year's figures with this year's)

conjunctions can start sentences. And this is an example. But don't overdo it.
- If you start a sentence with a conjunction like because or while, make it a complete sentence with a main clause, so avoid the following example. Because it's ungrammatical.

connection (not connexion)

contemporary: belonging to the same time/modern – use with care

continual (recurring with breaks) is confused with **continuous** (without a break)

courtesy titles: don't use Mr, Mrs, Miss, Ms, Mme, Mlle. Call people John Smith or Marie Duval the first time you refer to them, then John/Marie or Smith/Duval according to context

criteria is the plural of criterion

curate's egg: *see* **clichés**

currently: use **now**

cut (noun – not cutback) but to cut back

cuttings (press – not clippings)

data: use as both singular (not datum) and plural

dates: 20 March 1942 (no th or commas); the 1960s (no apostrophe)
- Don't combine from or between with a dash: write from 1940 to 1945, between 1940 and 1945 or 1940–45, not from 1940–45 or between 1940–1945

decimate: kill 1 in 10/destroy large numbers – don't use

deserts (runs away, sandy places, what is deserved) is confused with **desserts** (puddings)

détente: include accent

dexterous (not dextrous)

dicy (not dicey)

dice: use as both singular (not die) and plural

differ/different: use *from*, not *to* or *than*

dike (not dyke)

dilemma: use to mean awkward choice between two, not problem

discreet (prudent) is confused with **discrete** (separate)

disinterested: impartial/bored – don't use

disk for computers, **disc** for everything else

dispatch (not despatch)

dissociate (not disassociate)

dos and don'ts: only one apostrophe

dotcom (not dot-com, dot.com)

double negatives: avoid both the comic-colloquial (I don't know nothing about it) and the pompous (I am not unmindful of your wishes)

draft (sketch, money order)/**draught** (beer, depth for ships)

dreamt (not dreamed)

due to: must follow a noun or pronoun as in 'The cancellation was due to bad weather'. Instead of 'The train was cancelled due to bad weather' write 'The train was cancelled because of bad weather'

duffel (not duffle)

dwarfs (not dwarves) is the plural of dwarf

dying (a death)/**dyeing** (a jumper)

economic (about economics)/**economical** (thrifty)

effect: *see* **affect**

eg: comma before but not after

egregious: distinguished/notorious – don't use

email (not e-mail)

encyclopedia (not encyclopaedia)

ensure: *see* **assure**

envisage (not envision)

etc: no commas, no full stop

expatriate (not ex-patriot – unless they've stopped loving their country)

expat: don't use

fed up: with (not of)

fetus (not foetus)

fewer/less: if there are fewer trees there will be less wood

figures: *see* **numbers**

flaunt (display) is confused with **flout** (treat with contempt)

focused/focusing (not focussed/focussing)

folk, meaning people, also has the plural form folks; for the possessive use folks' (old folks' home)

following: if you mean after, use after

forbear (abstain)/**forebear** (ancestor)

forceful (energetic) is confused with **forcible** (done by force)

foreign words: *see* **franglais**. In general avoid words from other languages except French; if you have to use a non-French word, put it into italics. Don't put French words into italics

forego (go before)/**forgo** (do without)

format(verb)/**formatted/formatting**: use only for computers

formulas is the plural of formula

franglais: avoid misuses of French in English (eg embonpoint, which does not mean ample bosom) but, if appropriate, use French words that are current among local English-speaking people (eg bâche for tarpaulin, hangar for shed)

Frankenstein: *see* **clichés**

freelance (not freelancer)

further (not farther, even for distance)

gaff (hook to catch a fish, room or flat)/**gaffe** (blunder)

gay: use to mean homosexual, not light-hearted

geezer (bloke)/**geyser** (spring)

gender: *see* **sex**

geriatric: use to mean relating to care of the old, not old

graffiti is the plural of graffito

grey (not gray)

grisly (horrible)/**grizzly** (kind of bear)

handkerchiefs is the plural of handkerchief

hangar (shed)/**hanger** (for clothes)

hello (not hallo, hullo)

hiccup (not hiccough)

historic (famous)/**historical** (about history)

hi-tech (not high-tech)

hoard (hidden stock)/**horde** (multitude)

Hobson's choice: *see* **clichés**

hoi polloi (the plebs): don't use

holy (sacred)/**holey** (full of holes)

hopefully: by all means travel hopefully but don't write 'Hopefully we'll arrive tomorrow'

hurrah (not hooray) but Hooray Henry

hyphens: use them to make meaning clear: extra-marital sex; a black-cab driver/black cab-driver; a close-knit group. Do not use after -ly adverbs: instead prefer a closely knit group. When you hyphenate to mark word breaks, avoid a succession of hyphens and break words into their constituent parts. Avoid unintentional words, eg anal-ysis

I/me: prefer 'Fred and I were there' to 'Fred and me were there'; 'It's me' to 'It is I'; 'between you and me' to 'between you and I'

ie: comma before but not after

imply (suggest) is confused with **infer** (deduce)

inchoate: unformed/incoherent – don't use

infer: *see* **imply**

infinitives may be split by adverbs if necessary (It's difficult to really get to know somebody) but always ask yourself whether the adverb is necessary

initials: use people's first names unless they are publicly known by their initials; then set them in caps without full points or spaces: PD James. But note: ee cummings; kd lang

inquire/y (not enquire/y)

install/installation/instalment

instil/instillation/instilment

insure: *see* **assure**

-ise (not -ize) in all words except **capsize**

italics: use for the titles of newspapers, periodicals, books, plays, films, one-off broadcasts, serials and series. In newspaper titles 'The' stays in roman type, lower case, with the town or city of publication included for clarity: the London *Times*, the New York *Times*, the Portsmouth *News*, the Périgueux *News* etc. In periodical titles 'The' stays in roman type, lower case: the *Economist*, the *Journalist*. All other titles are given in full: *The Merchant of Venice*
- Also use italics *rarely* (rather than caps or screamers) for emphasis.
- Also *see* **foreign words**

jail (not gaol)

jargon: try to translate technical terms into English

jewellery (not jewelry)

John o'Groat's: keep the second apostrophe (it was originally John o'Groat's House)

judgment (not judgement)

laisser-faire (not laissez-faire)

lay/lie: lay the table and lie on the floor

leapt (not leaped)

learnt (as verb – not learned)

lend, to not to loan

less: *see* **fewer**

leukemia (not leukaemia)

lie: *see* **lay**

like: distinguish between the following:
1. like used to compare: Fruit trees are like flowers: they need water. Where appropriate, use commas to mark a parenthesis: Fruit trees, like flowers, need water.
2. like used instead of such as – don't use commas: Fruit trees like the cherry need pruning.
3. like used as a pause word in colloquial quotes (nowhere else) – do use commas: 'I'm, like, a singer'. (The speaker means they are a singer: take the commas away and it becomes a comparison.)

likeable (not likable)

linage (payment by the line)/**lineage** (ancestry)

linchpin (not lynchpin)

lovable (not loveable)

mantel/mantelpiece (above the fireplace)/**mantle** (cloak)

marijuana (not marihuana)

masterful (dominating) is confused with **masterly** (skilful)

may/might: 'First aid may have saved him' means that he may be alive. To show that we know he's dead, it must be: First aid might have saved him.

me: *see* **I**

media is the plural of medium meaning, eg the press

medieval (not mediaeval)

mediums is the plural of medium meaning spiritualist

metal (such as gold)/**mettle** (courage)

meter (gauge)/**metre** (measure)

might: *see* **may**

mileage (not milage)

militate (contend) is confused with **mitigate** (soften)

movable (not moveable except in Hemingway's 'A Moveable Feast')

Muslim (not Moslem)

naivety (not naiveté)

no one: not no-one

none takes either a singular or a plural verb; the plural often sounds more natural: 'None of our problems have been solved'

nosy (not nosey)

numbers: one to nine are written as words and figures start at 10; but 9–10, not nine-10
- Percentages are always in figures: 6.5 per cent; 1 per cent
- For time use the 24-hour clock: the meeting will be at 18h/18h30
- Figures above 999 take commas: 1,760
- Decimals take a full point: 17.6

OK (not okay)

only should go as near as possible to the word or phrase it refers to: 'She arrived only last week. But we can live with 'I'm only here for the beer'

orientate (not orient)

paediatrician/paedophile (not pediatrician/pedophile)

participles: when dangling, watch your participles. This is the commonest – and worst – mistake in modern journalism. 'Born in Brixton, his father was a trapeze artist.' Who?

pedaller (cyclist)/**pedlar** (hawker)/**peddler** (drug dealer)

people is mainly used as the plural of person (the people's champion) but it is also used as a singular noun to mean nation; then its plural is peoples (possessive peoples')

phenomena is the plural of phenomenon

phoney (not phony)

prepositions can end sentences – what else are you thinking of?

prescribe (lay down) is confused with **proscribe** (prohibit)

pressurise (not pressure) as verb

prevaricate (evade the truth) is confused with **procrastinate** (defer action)

preventive (not preventative)

pricy (not pricey)

principal (main or head)/**principle** (basis)

pristine: original/new – don't use

processor (not processer)

procrastinate: *see* **prevaricate**

program for computers, **programme** for everything else

proscribe: *see* **prescribe**

protagonist: chief actor/any person or character/person in favour – don't use

protester (not protestor)

queries (question marks): include after rhetorical questions

quotes: in text use single quotes with double inside single; in headlines use single quotes
- Please don't start stories with quotes
- Introduce full-sentence quotes with a colon not a comma
- Edit quotes when necessary (a) to shorten (b) to clarify (c) to remove bad grammar, but *never* change the meaning

race: only mention race where it is relevant; in general use the descriptions people use of themselves. Terms include Afro-Caribbean, Asian, black, mixed race, Romany, white
- In general use caps for geographically based terms; but distinguish between Gypsy for specific groups of Romany people and gypsy for general references to an outdoor, unconventional way of life

realise (not realize)

rebut: deny, argue against, show to be false – don't use

redundancy/repetition/saying it twice/tautology: whatever you call it don't write 'They were both talking to each other'

refute: deny, show to be false – don't use

register (not registry) **office** for marriage

regularly: use to mean at regular intervals, not often

relative/relation (for family): use either – but not both close together

religion: use caps for Anglican, Baptist, Buddhist, Catholic (not Roman Catholic), Christian, Jewish, Muslim, Protestant etc
- Give Anglican clerics their courtesy title the first time you refer to them: the Rev John/Mary Smith. Then call them John/Mary or Smith according to context; never call anyone the Rev Smith

repetition: see **redundancy**

reticent: use to mean reluctant to speak, not reluctant to act

review (critical notice)/**revue** (theatrical show)

rise (in prices – not hike)

saying it twice: *see* **redundancy**

screamers (! ! !): avoid

sensual (physically gratifying) is confused with **sensuous** (affecting the senses)

sex/gender: gender is a grammatical term; to distinguish between men and women prefer the word sex
- Don't use male terms generically: say police officers not policemen, fire-fighters not firemen. But for individuals use spokesman/spokeswoman, chairman/chairwoman; don't use spokesperson, chairperson etc

- For female actors use actress – also abbess, countess, duchess, goddess, marchioness – but not poetess, sculptress etc

singing (a song)/**singeing** (a beard)

smelt (not smelled)

smidgen (not smidgeon)

spelling: use British not American spelling
  - For words not given in this style guide follow Chambers (not Collins, Longmans, Oxford, Penguin and certainly not Webster's), using the first spelling given

spelt (not spelled)

spicy (not spicey)

spoilt (not spoiled)

stadiums is the plural of stadium

story (tale)/**storey** (in building)

straitjacket (not straightjacket)

sufficient: use enough

swap (not swop)

swinging (from a tree)/**swingeing** (savage)

tautology: *see* **redundancy**

that/which: This is the house that Jack built (defines, no commas); Jack's house, which he bought last year, is worth £1 million (adds extra information, commas)

they is better than he/she and he or she if the sex of the person is not specified: Anyone can come if they want to

tortuous (difficult) is confused with **torturous** (like torture)

trade (not trades) **union** but **Trades Union Congress**

trade names: unless a trade name is important to the story, always use an equivalent term, eg vacuum cleaner for Hoover, ballpoint pen for Biro, photocopier for Xerox (see list of trade names below)

transatlantic (not transAtlantic)

tsar (not czar)

T-shirt (not tee-shirt)

tyre (not tire)

verbal: use to mean spoken (as in verbal agreement)

wagon (not waggon)

wagons-lits is the plural of wagon-lit

waiver (renunciation)/**waver** (vacillate)

which: *see* **that**

while (not whilst)

whisky (not whiskey – unless Irish or American is specified)

who/whom: in general prefer 'Who did you invite?' to 'Whom did you invite?'
    Never write 'Whom did you say was there?'

Trade names

adidas (lower-case a): sportswear
Ansafone: answering machine
Aspro: aspirin analgesic
Autocue: teleprompter

Biro: ballpoint pen
Burberry: mackintosh

Calor: bottled gas
Caterpillar: continuous-tread vehicle
Cellophane: cellulose film
Coca-Cola: cola drink
Courtelle: acrylic fibre
Crimplene: polyester filament yarn

Dacron: polyester fibre
Dettol: antiseptic disinfectant
Dictaphone: dictating machine
Dinky: miniature toy vehicle
Distalgesic: analgesic
Dolby: noise-reduction circuitry
Dormobile: minibus
Dralon: acrylic fibre
Dunlopillo: resilient foam
Dymo: embossing tool, tape

Elastoplast: sticking plaster

Fibreglass: glass fibre
Flymo: hover mower
Formica: laminate

Hoover: vacuum cleaner

Instamatic: cartridge camera

Jacuzzi: whirlpool bath
Jiffy bag: postal bag

KiloStream: digital communications
Kleenex: paper tissues

Land Rover: all-purpose vehicle
Lego: interlocking toy bricks
Letraset: dry transfer lettering
Levi's: jeans

Meccano: assembly-kit toy
MegaStream: digital communications

Nescafé: instant coffee

Orlon: acrylic fibre

Pentothal: barbiturate for anaesthesia
Perspex: acrylic sheet
Photostat: photocopier/y
Plasticine: modelling clay
Polaroid: filter, camera, sunglasses
Portakabin: portable building
Primus: stove, heater
Pyrex: heat-resistant glass

Range Rover: all-purpose vehicle

Scotch Tape: transparent adhesive tape
Sellotape: transparent adhesive tape
Spam: chopped pork and ham

Teflon: non-stick coating on pans
Terylene: polyester fibre
Thermos: vacuum flask
Triplex: safety glass

Vaseline: petroleum jelly
Velcro: press-together fastening

Xerox: photocopier

Yellow Pages: business telephone directory

Appendix 2
Billy the Kid, the left-handed gunman who wasn't

The readers' editor on ... the left-handed gunman who wasn't

I kid you not

Ian Mayes

Open door

Not long ago, when our Washington correspondent filed a report of moves in the United States to secure a posthumous pardon for Billy the Kid, we illustrated the story with a photograph of the famous outlaw. This is a ferrotype, or tintype, probably taken in 1880, the year he was captured by Sheriff Pat Garrett.

The photograph, familiar to all students of the West, but less so to the rest of us, shows Billy the Kid, full-length, the butt of his Winchester resting on the ground and the tip of the barrel gripped lightly in his right hand. More to the point, he carries his single-action Colt on his left hip, the handle pointing backwards. To everyone involved in editing the page on which it appeared, everything seemed as it should be. Wasn't Billy, after all, a notorious left-hander – played as such by Paul Newman in Arthur Penn's 1958 film The Left-Handed Gun?

Almost immediately after the Guardian report appeared, I received an email from a reader: "Your reproduction of the famous photograph of Billy the Kid is reversed. You can see by the waistcoat buttons and the belt buckle. This is a common error which has continued to reinforce the myth that Billy the Kid was left-handed. He was not. He was right-handed and carried his gun on his right hip." The writer of the email was, it transpired, a former curator of the National Film and Television Archive of the British Film Institute, Clyde Jeavons.

His points about the buckle and buttons were indeed borne out on closer examination. The prong on the belt buckle is pointing the wrong way, and the buttons run down the wrong side of his waistcoat. There is no doubt that what we are looking at is a reverse image.

Was it simply another case of "flipping the picture"? After all, we have in the past presented readers of the Guardian with a photograph of an entirely left-handed orchestra and a flipped image of the Horsehead nebula. This case, however, did not prove so simple.

My correspondent produced further argument. "This particular reproduction error has occurred so often in books and other publications over the years that it has led to the myth that Billy the Kid was left-handed, for which there is no evidence. On the contrary, the evidence (from viewing his photo correctly) is that he was right-handed: he wears his pistol on his right hip with the butt pointing backwards in a conventional right-handed draw position."

He cites the Pictorial History of the Wild West by James D Horan and Paul Sann, 1954, in which the authors caption the "correctly printed" picture: "Billy the Kid. He was right-handed and carried his pistol on his right hip."

Edward Buscombe, in The BFI Companion to the Western, 1988, now sadly out of print, while not commenting directly on the left hand/right hand issue, says this: "There has probably been more tedious argument about the facts of Billy the Kid's life than about anything else in the West." Alongside he prints the photograph to show the gun on Billy's right hip (buttons and buckle all in order) – the reverse of the Guardian's presentation.

A quick internet search produces vast quantities of information, including sites devoted to Billy the Kid which reproduce the image in question, usually showing it, as it appeared in the Guardian, with the pistol on the right of the picture – that is, on his left hip, if you regard it as you would a modern photograph.

The answer, in fact, is in the technique used to obtain the image in the first place. The tintype or ferrotype, to quote Britannica.com, was "a positive photograph produced by means of a nitrocellulose (collodion) solution applied to a thin enamelled black iron plate immed-iately prior to exposure". It says they remained a kind of folk art for the rest of the 19th century.

The best description I have found is in the online work, A History of Photography, compiled by Robert Leggat (www. rleggat.com/photohistory/). He makes the following essential point: "The print would come out laterally reversed (as one sees oneself in a mirror); either people did not worry about this, or just possibly they did not discover it until after the photographer had disappeared!"

So the "authentic" tintype of Billy the Kid, if one is to be purist about this, should be shown as it appeared in the Guardian, but pointing out that the image is reversed. If we want to see Billy the Kid the right way round, we have to grit our teeth, break our own rule forbidding the flipping of pictures, and reverse it again.

If you are still with me, the essential point in all this is that Billy the Kid was not, on the evidence of this image, left-handed. I find myself on the side of the right.

The Guardian carried the picture of Billy the Kid on February 3. Special thanks to Clyde Jeavons, who provided me with a good deal of the material for this column; and to Edward Buscombe. A key book is Billy the Kid: A Short and Violent Life by Robert M. Utley, University of Nebraska Press, 1989. Readers may contact the office of the readers' editor by telephoning 020–7239 9589 between 11am and 5pm, Monday to Friday. Mail to Readers' editor, The Guardian, 119 Farringdon Road, London EC1R 3ER. Fax 020–7239 9897. Email: reader@guardian.co.uk

Appendix 3
British proof correction symbols

Instruction	Textual mark	Marginal mark
Leave unchanged	_ _ _ _ under characters	⊘
Remove extraneous marks	Encircle marks to be removed	✕
Delete	/ through character(s) or ⊢⊣ through words	♪
Delete and close up	⨍ through character(s) or ⊟	♪
Insert in text the matter indicated in the margin	⋏	New matter followed by ⋏
Substitute character or substitute part of one or more words	/ through character or ⊢⊣ hrough word(s)	New character or new word(s)
Substitute ligature e.g. æ for separate letters	⊢⊣ through characters affected	⌢ e.g. æ̂
Substitute or insert full stop or decimal point	/ through character or ⋏	⊙
Substitute or insert comma, semicolon, colon, etc.	/ through character or ⋏	,/;/⊙/(/)/
Substitute or insert character in 'superior' position	/ through character or ⋏	⌐ under character e.g. ²⌐
Substitute or insert character in 'inferior' position	/ through character or ⋏	∟ over character e.g. ₂∟
Substitute or insert single or double quotation marks or apostrophe	/ through character or ⋏	⁊ ⁊̈ and/or ⁊ ⁊̈
Substitute or insert ellipsis	/ through character or ⋏	. . .
Substitute or insert hyphen	/ through character or ⋏	⊢=⊣
Substitute or insert rule	/ through character or ⋏	Give the size of the rule in the marginal mark ⊢1 em⊣ ⊢4 mm⊣

Instruction	Textual mark	Marginal mark
Substitute or insert oblique	/ through character or ⋏	Ⓘ
Wrong fount. Replace by character(s) of correct fount	Encircle character(s)	⊗
Change damaged character(s)	Encircle character(s)	✕
Set in or change to italic	—— under character(s) Where space does not permit textual marks, encircle the affected area instead	⊔
Change italic to upright type	Encircle character(s)	⊔
Set in or change to capital letters	≡≡≡ under character(s)	≡
Set in or change to small capital letters	=== under character(s)	=
Set in or change to bold type	∿∿∿ under character(s)	∿
Set in or change to bold italic type	∿∿∿ under character(s)	⊔∿
Change capital letters to lower-case letters	Encircle character(s)	⌗
Change small capital letters to lower-case letters	Encircle character(s)	⌗
Close up. Delete space between characters or words	⌒ linking characters ⌣ e.g. a⌢scribe	⌒⌣
Insert space between characters	| between characters	Υ Give the size of the space when necessary
Insert space between words	Υ between words	Υ Give the size of the space when necessary
Reduce space between characters	| between characters	⋀ Give the amount by which the space is to be reduced, when necessary

Instruction	Textual mark	Marginal mark
Reduce space between words	⌐ between words	Give the amount by which the space is to be reduced, when necessary
Make space appear equal between characters or words	| between characters or words	
Close up to normal interline spacing	(each side of column linking lines)	
Insert space between lines or paragraphs	or	Give the size of the space when necessary
Reduce space between lines or paragraphs	or	Give amount by which the space is to be reduced, when necessary
Start new paragraph		
Run on (no new paragraph)		
Transpose characters or words	between characters or words, numbered when necessary	
Transpose lines		
Transpose a number of lines	3 2 1	Rules extend from the margin into the text with each line to be transposed numbered in the correct sequence
Centre	⌐enclosing matter⌐ to be centred	[ ]
Indent		Give the amount of the indent
Cancel indent		
Move matter specified distance to the right*	enclosing matter to be moved to the right	

Instruction	Textual mark	Marginal mark
Move matter specified distance to the left*	enclosing matter to be moved to the left	
Set line to specified measure*	and/or	
Set column to specified measure*		
Take over character(s), word(s) or line to next line, column or page		The textual mark surrounds the matter to be taken over and extends into the margin
Take back character(s), word(s) or line to previous line, column or page		The textual mark surrounds the matter to be taken back and extends into the margin
Raise matter*	over matter to be raised / under matter to be raised	
Lower matter*	over matter to be lowered / under matter to be lowered	
Move matter to position indicated*	Enclose matter to be moved and indicate new position	
Correct vertical alignment		
Correct horizontal alignment	Single line above and below misaligned matter	placed level with the head and foot of the relevant line

* Give the exact dimensions when necessary.

Appendix 4
US proof correction symbols

EXAMPLE OF MARKED PROOF

⌐ Authors As Proofreaders ⌐   *ctr /lc*

flush
⌐ "I don't care what kind of type you use for my
book," said a myopic author to the publisher, but please   ℘
print the galley proofs in large type. Perhaps in the   ℘
future such a request will not sound so ridiculous ⌐   ⌐
i   to those familar with the printing process. Today,   *cap*
however, type once set is not reset exepct to correct   *tr*
errors.[1]

1. Type may be reduced in size, or enlarged photographically when a   ↗
book is printed by offset.

Proofreading is an Art and a craft. All authors   *lc /stet*
should know the rudiments thereof, though no   ⌃
proofreader expects them to be masters of it. Watch
proofreader expects them to be masters of it. Watch   *d*
not only for misspelled or incorrect works (often a   *d*
e/)   most illusive error, but also for misplaced spaces, "un-   *c/#*
tr   closde" quotation marks and parenthesis, and im-   *eq. # /e*
tr   porper paragraphing; and learn to recognize the
difference between an em dash—used to separate an
interjectional part of a sentence—and an en dash used
tr   commonly between continuing numbers (e.g., pp.   ✗
⊇/sc/lc   5–10; a.d. 1165/70) and the word dividing hyphen.   )=/
Sometimes, too, a letter from a wrong font will creep   *wf*
tr/⊙   a mathematical formula. Whatever is underlined in   *rom*
into the printed text, or a boldface k or d turn up in   *ital /H*
op |↗   a MS. should, of course, be italicized in print. To find
the errors overlooked by the proofreader is the
authors first problem in proof reading. The sec-   ⊃
ond problem is to make corrections using the marks   *-by*
s/   and symbols, devized by proffessional proofreaders,
that any trained typesetter will understand. The
third—and most difficult problem for authors proof-   ⅟₄
reading their own works is to resist the temptation to
=   rewrite in proofs.

Manuscript editor   □   *c+sc/* □

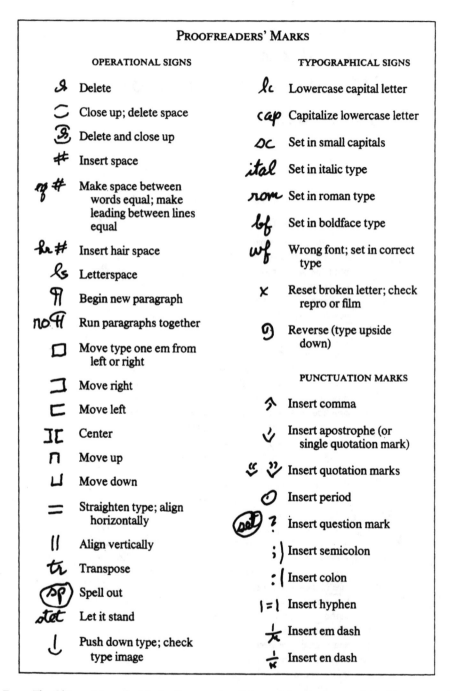

PROOFREADERS' MARKS

OPERATIONAL SIGNS

ℐ	Delete
⌒	Close up; delete space
ℬ	Delete and close up
#	Insert space
eq #	Make space between words equal; make leading between lines equal
hr #	Insert hair space
ls	Letterspace
¶	Begin new paragraph
no ¶	Run paragraphs together
☐	Move type one em from left or right
⊐	Move right
⊏	Move left
⊐⊏	Center
⊓	Move up
⊔	Move down
=	Straighten type; align horizontally
‖	Align vertically
tr	Transpose
(sp)	Spell out
stet	Let it stand
⌄	Push down type; check type image

TYPOGRAPHICAL SIGNS

lc	Lowercase capital letter
cap	Capitalize lowercase letter
sc	Set in small capitals
ital	Set in italic type
rom	Set in roman type
bf	Set in boldface type
wf	Wrong font; set in correct type
x	Reset broken letter; check repro or film
↺	Reverse (type upside down)

PUNCTUATION MARKS

⋀	Insert comma
∨	Insert apostrophe (or single quotation mark)
⸌⸍	Insert quotation marks
⊙	Insert period
(∘∘∘) ?	Insert question mark
;	Insert semicolon
:	Insert colon
‖=‖	Insert hyphen
⊥	Insert em dash
⊥	Insert en dash

From *The Chicago Manual of Style*, Fourteenth edition, with permission of the University of Chicago Press.

Index